M...

A Baby In A Manger

by Larry Rice

More Than A Baby In A Manger

By Larry Rice

Saint Louis, Missouri

Introduction

To help you celebrate this Christmas the following inspirational messages are being shared with you. In them you will find a variety of explanations concerning the birth of Christ that you may not have encountered before. These include joining Creation in the Celebration of Christmas, Divine Love Making, the symbols and timing of Christmas and more.

The cover is a picture of my two dear sisters, Carolyn and Shirley taken in 1957. Christmas was such a special time for the Rice family in which many fond memories were created.

I pray that this book will be a blessing this Christmas in your life and in the lives of those you share it with. As you read this book you will see that Christmas is more than a baby in a manger. It is God fulfilling His covenant to redeem His creation. This redemptive act provides hope both now and for eternity by sending Jesus who is truly the reason for the season.

—Larry Rice

The Rice Family
1969

More Than A Baby In A Manger

Chapter One- Christmas Memories

The word Christmas has a way of sparking memories in the hearts and minds of all of us. Some of these memories may be more pleasant than others.

I remember as a child how every Christmas Eve my brother and sisters and I would be in a Christmas Pageant at the church. After it was over, we were given paper bags of fruit and candy as we left the church. Then when we got home, we would open our presents.

Larry with his sisters Carolyn, Shirley, and brother Kenneth.

One year when my children were growing up, we decided to celebrate Christmas with a family in East St. Louis. This family had their home broken into and two of the children had been shot. During our celebration, while we were videotaping, a light blew out with a loud pop. All the children we were visiting started to run for cover thinking it was gunfire. Even with that bit of drama it was still a memorable Christmas as the children all learned to share and express the Christmas Spirit.

What Christmas memories do you have? Are they delightful or depressing? Some have said Christmas is the celebration of the birth of Christ, but they remain depressed because they give more attention to Santa Claus than they do Jesus Christ. What do you find gives you the greatest memories about Christmas? In order to discover the answer to that question we must turn to Matthew Chapters 1-2, and Luke 1-2.

In Matthew 1:21 we see that the best Christmas memory available is that Jesus was born, and He will "save His people from their sins." The reality of this fact offers hope to those who realize that all have sinned and fallen short of the glory of God (Romans 3:23). Yet even though we were sinners destined to hell, God loved us and came among us. The realization of this results in a memory of Christmas that is one of praise and thanksgiving.

Listen to this Christmas memory as it is reflected in Matthew 1:23, which declares that Isaiah 7:14 has been fulfilled. "The virgin will be with child and will give birth to a son, and they will call him Immanuel – which means, 'God with us'".

The reality of Christmas results in worship, because we are no longer alone for "God is with us." We can start believing that things are going to change for the better because God loves us so much "that He gave His one and only Son,

Christmas at the
Cervantes Center in 1993

that whoever believes in Him shall not perish but have eternal life" (John 3:16).

Just like the wise men, we have every reason to rejoice for, "When they saw the star, they were overjoyed. On coming to the house, they saw the child with His mother Mary, and they bowed down and worshipped Him. Then they opened their treasures and presented Him with gifts of gold and of frankincense and of myrrh" (Matthew 2:10-11).

Mary expressed the fact that "His (God's) mercy extends to those who fear Him, from generation to generation. He has performed mighty deeds with His arm; He has scattered those who are proud in their inmost thoughts. He has brought down rulers from their thrones but has lifted up the humble. He has filled the hungry with good things but has sent the rich away empty" (Luke 1:50-53).

My best memories about Christmas involve New Life Evangelistic Center feeding the poor and homeless each Christmas Day. As this is done, they are reminded of the special love God has for them.

Zechariah declares in Luke 1:78-79 that the real meaning of Christmas involves letting the rising sun of Jesus shine on us until we are delivered from darkness. This happens "because of the tender mercy of our God, with which the sunrise from on high will visit us from heaven to shine on those who sit in darkness and the shadow of death to guide our feet into the way of peace."

The angels proclaimed this path of peace when they declared, "Glory to God in the highest heaven, and on earth peace to men (and women) on whom His favor rests" (Luke 2:14).

Once the shepherds experienced this joyful proclamation of the angels, they took direct action to proceed to first seek the source of the spirit of Christmas, the Christ child and then they told everyone about Him (Luke 2:17-18).

When Simeon saw the baby Jesus, he was moved by the Spirit and declared, "For my eyes have seen your salvation, which you have prepared in the sight of all nations: a light for revelation to the Gentiles, and the glory of your people Israel" (Luke 2:29-32).

Eighty-four-year-old Anna after seeing Jesus also gave thanks to God and told everyone about the child. Experiencing the Christ of Christmas causes us to engage in the direct action of sharing in word and deed the hope that the spirit of Christmas provides. Such sharing creates within us Christmas memories that last a lifetime.

Developing positive Christmas memories involves taking a different route like the wise men did. "And having been warned in a dream not to go back to Herod, they returned to their country by another route" (Matthew 2:12).

Taking a different route involves having our eyes opened so we can truly see and appreciate the Christ child. Jesus said in Matthew 13:16, "blessed are your eyes because they see, and your ears because they hear."

When our eyes of faith are opened, we are assured in the depths of our soul that no matter what the circumstances may dictate we do not need to be afraid. Joseph, after being told this in Matt. 1:20, believed, and God provided for him. In this case God used the wise men to share gifts to finance Joseph, Mary and the baby Jesus' trip to Egypt "where he stayed until the death of Herod" (Matt. 2:15). In the same way you can also truly celebrate life when you choose not to fear but instead go forth by faith.

In Luke 1:13 we see Zechariah being told to not be afraid. Mary is told the same thing in Luke 1:30, "Do not be afraid, Mary, you have found favor with God".

Positive Christmas memories involve allowing the spirit of Faith to replace the spirit of Fear.

The reason you and I don't have to be afraid is because we have found favor with God. This favor is grace, and it is not a result of anything we have done. It is God's free gift coming from His infinite love. It is not for us to question this un-merited favor but to celebrate the fact that it exists because "Nothing will be impossible with God" (Luke 1:37 ESV).

Just as Mary celebrated Christmas and declared, "Behold the handmaid of the Lord; be it with me according to thy word" (Luke 1:38), we also need to let Christ be born with-in us. 2 Corinthians 5:17 declares, "Therefore, if anyone is in Christ, the new creation has come: the old has gone, the new is here" (2 Cor. 5:17).

When the re-creation has taken place in our lives we will join Mary and declare, "My soul glorifies the Lord and my spirit rejoices in God my Savior, for He has been mindful of the humble state of His servant. From now on all genera-tions will call me blessed, for the Mighty One has done great things for me-holy is His name" (Luke 1:46-49).

This Christmas let's truly celebrate for, "Christ has brought down rulers from their thrones but has lifted up the humble. He has filled the hungry with good things but has sent the rich away empty" (Luke 1:52, 53).

Instead of fearing the uncertainty of the future now is the time to step out in faith. As we do this, we can accept God's promise "to rescue us from the hand of our enemies, and to enable us to serve Him without fear" (Luke 1:73, 74).

Jesus Christ was born a homeless child and placed in a manger, "because there was no guest room available for them" (Luke 2:7). The greatest memories of Christmas take place when we make room in our heart for Jesus by reach-ing out and helping those in need. As we do this, we will begin to understand what the angel meant when he de-clared to the shepherds, "Do not be afraid. I bring you good news that will cause great joy for all the people. Today in the town of David a Savior has been born to you; He is the Messiah, the Lord" (Luke 2:10, 11).

The best Christmas memories take place when we realize that in the midst of our sinfulness and hopelessness Jesus has arrived and has provided the means of salvation.

The angels realizing that the miracle birth of the Christ child was about to take place proceeded to give the shepherds that great celestial show when, "suddenly a great company of the heavenly host appeared with the angel, praising God, and saying, 'Glory to God in the highest, and on earth peace to those on whom His favor rests" (Luke 2:14).

There is hope both now and for all eternity because our Savior has come. He is more than a baby in a manger. This realization touches every aspect of our lives. Now we can declare, "Thank you Father that I have your favor through Jesus Christ. I am no longer a victim because you have made me a victor. Your favor is opening for me doors of opportunity both now and throughout all eternity."

This year strive to make positive Christmas memories. Don't take God's blessing of the Living Christ for granted. Thank Him for Jesus and spread the word concerning the true meaning of Christmas. Celebrate the fact the Savior has come and now, "with minds that are alert and fully sober, set your hope on the grace to be brought to you when Jesus Christ is revealed at His coming" (I Peter 1:13).

At this moment you may not have any positive Christmas memories. Job in his loneliest, darkest hours of sickness and affliction cried out, "God I know that you have granted me favor" (John 10:12). He made that statement of faith in chapter 10 even though he was not healed until chapter 42.

Simeon an old man in the temple did not experience the resurrected Christ as you and I can today, yet "Simeon took Him (as a little baby) in his arms and praised God, saying: 'Sovereign Lord, as you have promised, you may now dismiss your servant in peace. For my eyes have seen your salvation, which you have prepared in the sight of all nations" (Luke 2:28-31).

Now let the Lord fill your eyes, ears, mind and heart with Christmas memories that will last a lifetime. Jesus tells us that "According to your faith let it be done to you" (Matthew 9:29).

Stop living in fear and unbelief. A Savior has come. Celebrate the new beginning He has given. Let it be done to you according to your faith.

If you refuse to be afraid and instead celebrate the faith and favor God has provided through Jesus Christ, you will automatically start developing Christmas memories that will last a lifetime.

Chris Aaron, Irene, and Abigail

Kenneth, Lowie and Maggie (the dog)

Chapter Two: Joining Creation in the Celebration of Christmas

Sheep, donkeys, cattle, camels, and other animals in creation join angels, stars, and heavenly hosts in the celebration of God becoming man and dwelling amongst us. This event which we celebrate as Christmas is the pivotal point, not only in human history, but the life of every animal, plant, bird or living creature that has suffered at the hands of sinful human beings.

John 3:16 tells us that, "For God so loved the world (cosmos), (his total creation on planet Earth), that He gave His one and only Son that whoever believes in Him shall not perish but have eternal life".

"Do Not be afraid, I bring you good tidings of great joy, for unto you is born this day in the city of David, Christ the Lord."
Luke 2:10

This giving by the divine creator of life provides hope not only for humanity but all of creation. With eager expectation the donkey carries Mary to Bethlehem sensing that the woman he was carrying is about to give birth. With alarm the sheep are aroused from their sleep as the sky becomes lit up with an array of heavenly hosts. Then, one of the angels proclaimed, "Do not be afraid, I bring you good news that will cause great joy for all the people" (Luke 2:10).

As the sheep stared into the sky with amazement suddenly the heavenly host broke into praise singing, "Glory to God in the highest heaven, and on earth peace to those on whom His favor rests."

By this time the flock should be ready to bolt, but a divine calm settles over them and with great anticipation they move toward Bethlehem under the direction of their shepherds.

Filling the quiet streets of Bethlehem, ewes, rams and lambs still in awe of what they had just seen, move slowly as if guided by the hand of God to a stable that exists in a cave next to the inn. Along with the cattle and other livestock in attendance they crowd around a simple manger in which lies a child that they know is no ordinary child.

He is the homeless child that every animal which has ever been mistreated by the sinful hands of man has longed for. Paul put it this way in Romans 8:20, 21, "For the creation was subjected to frustration, not by its own choice, but by the will of the one who subjected it, in hope that the creation itself will be liberated from its bondage to decay and brought into the freedom and glory of the children of God.

The baby in that manger, the incarnation of the living God, would be the Redeemer of all humanity. He would

The virgin will be with child and will give birth to a son, and they will call him Immanuel - which means, 'God with us"
Matthew 1:23.

be the one who made it possible for greedy, self-serving human beings to be made new creations of love. In this manger surrounded by the animals God created, existed the hope for all of creation, which had been subjected to frustration because of the sins of humanity. It would be this child and his future death and resurrection which would provide the antidote to the cancer of sin and the worldwide frustration it created. This baby, who was fully God and man, is called in Matthew 1:23, "Immanuel...'God with us'".

In order to appreciate the miracle of creation, we must ask

the Holy Spirit to enable us to see not just animals, birds, people and the rest of created life as a group, but also recognize the wisdom and beauty in each created form of life. For example, in Genesis 1:20 it says, "And God said, 'Let the water teem with living creatures, and let birds fly above the earth across the vault of the sky.'"

Looking at just one of the living creatures in the water, the dolphins, shows a fish that has a brain that instantaneously calculates the nature of the surrounding environment from the re-

"And God said, "Let the water teem with living creatures, and let birds fly above the earth across the expanse of the sky.'" Genesis 1:20

verberations from the ultrasounds produced by a specialized organ in the front of its skull (200,000 vibrations per second).

Observe for a moment a flock of geese and their V-shape formation as they fly through the sky. The leader, the strongest bird, uses his strength to shield the birds following from opposing air currents, enabling the entire flock to gain an improved efficiency and speed of up to 23%.

Volumes could be written on the very subject of examining the miraculous in each particular species. Humanity, which Genesis 1:27 speaks of being created in the image of God, has the ability to also create and reflect on the purpose and meaning of life. Dr. Isaac Asimov wrote, "In man is a three-pound brain which, as far as we know, is the most complex and orderly arrangement of matter in the universe." This brain is given the opportunity to make decisions and

when the decisions violate God's estab-lished order, sin is the result.

The scene changed in Genesis 3 when humani-ty's rebelliousness against the Creator results in sin's pol-lution of creation. Man and woman, made in the image of God, have tarnished this image, and upon being evicted from the Garden, they find themselves in a hope-less situation until God intervenes with His promise of a Savior (Genesis 3:15).

It is the fulfillment of this promise that all creation celebrates at Christmas. Without the celebration of the blessings of Christ-mas it will be a time of stress and depression for every living crea-ture. The real blessing of Christmas is the coming of the Messiah, Jesus Christ, whose life, death, and resurrection fills the hunger to be restored to God and to His creation.

Colossians 1:15-17 illustrates the fulfillment that can take place through the Christ of Christmas. "The Son is the image of the invisible God, the first-born over-all creation. For in Him all things were created: things in heaven and on earth, visible and invisible, whether thrones or powers or rulers or authorities: all things have been created through Him and for Him. He is before all things, and in Him all things hold together."

Jonathan Edwards, experiencing a great spiritual awakening, believed that God made it possible for humans through Jesus Christ to be recreated in God's image. As this happens their spiritual eyes are opened, and they are able to participate deeply and inwardly in the  beauty of nature. Edwards stated, "God's excellency, His wisdom, His purity and love seemed to appear in everything, in the sun, moon and stars; in the clouds and blue sky; in the grass, flowers trees, in the water, and all nature."

The one who experiences the Christ of Christmas only theoretically or emotionally is the one who usually remains quiet in the midst of environmental terrorism. The true believers in resurrection and life will speak out when they hear that a species is destroyed every 8 hours, that the earth's oxygen is rapidly being depleted by the felling of 25 million acres of rain forestry each year, and that carbon dioxide is being pumped into the air at record rates by utility companies totally dependent on fossil fuels.

 At Christmas not only humanity but all creation is given God's gift of His Son. It is Jesus who provides the miracle of redemption resulting in the re-creation of a sin driven humanity. The recreated are a people who work to preserve all of creation for

they realize creation does not exist for mankind alone but for the Living God. They are a people who have been redeemed to live for His glory. This means they are an involved people filled with hope.

This hope is personified in the child, who is the Lamb of God, who takes away the sin of the world. Jesus is also the Lion of Judah, who will someday return triumphant in all His glory. It is this hope that all creation celebrates.

"Weep No more, behold the Lion of the tribe of Judah the root of David has conquered..."
Revelation 5:5

Chapter 3: Music from Creation and Heaven

Can you hear the music of creation? It is heard in the harmony of all that God has created. The music of creation is the music of Christmas.

If we are serious about worshipping God and getting a deeper under-standing of the message of Christmas, then we should start listening a little closer to the music of creation. This music is heard in the chirping of the birds, the insects, the wind blowing through the trees and so much more.

As God takes John to heaven, He immerses him in the music of creation (see Revelation 4 & 5). Heaven is a place of perfect harmony, un-touched by human sin. In the center of this worship music

of creation John is intro-duced to the four living creatures. "The first living creature was like a lion, the second was like an ox, the third had the face of a man, the fourth was like a flying eagle" (Revelation 4:7).

These four living creatures represent the balance that the Christ of Christmas brings to us as we join the rest of creation in praising God.

Two out of four of these creatures come from the animal kingdom, the third is a bird which combines with the fourth, a man to provide the perfect music of creation.

The lion like the lion of Judah shows the boldness that comes into the lives of those who receive the Christ of Christmas. The ox, which was at the first Christmas, shows the perseverance and steadfastness that Jesus brings into our lives. The man symbolizes the compassion and caring that the Christ of Christmas gives to those who follow Him. The eagle represents the angels and how we can, through Christ rise above our problems victoriously as prayer warriors.

The four living creatures reveal the harmony that can take place in our personal lives as we receive the Christ of Christmas. "Each of the four living creatures had six wings and was covered with eyes all around even under his wings. Day and night they never stop saying: 'Holy, holy, holy is the Lord God Almighty, who was, and is, and is to come'" (Revelation 4:8).

On earth the music of creation is also heard. The problem is the harmony of creations music has been destroyed by sin. The antidote for this poison of sin is provided through the death and resurrection of the Christ of Christmas. All of creation knows this as John further reveals what he saw when he visited heaven. "Then I heard every creature in heaven and on earth and under the earth and on the sea and all that is in them singing: 'To Him who sits on the throne and to the Lamb be praise and honor and glory and power, forever and ever'" (Revelation 5:13).

This revelation that John shares with us makes it clear that Christ's redemptive

work goes far beyond just humanity but includes all of creation. Look at the nativity scene, it doesn't just involve people but also animals.

That is why John heard every creature in heaven and on earth and under the earth and on the sea and all that is in them singing.

The music of creation is all around us. From the whale deep within the ocean to the ram on the highest mountaintop and the bird in the limb of the tree, Psalm 150:6 says, "Let everything that has breath praise the Lord."

Many who see only a baby in a manger at Christmas miss out on experiencing the music of creation. This is a result of the fact that their world is primarily made up of asphalt, computers, and fluorescent lighting.

Elizabeth Achtemeir in her book entitled Nature, God and Pulpit says, "There are thousands of people in our cities who have never seen a cow, and who could not say if the stars were out because city lights and smog block their

vision. A youth leader in New York City took his teenage group into the country and found to his amazement that they were terrified when they saw a deer. The natural world has become strange to us, divorced from our thoughts and vocabu-

lary, so that few sermons anymore use natural images – a development that has impoverished our language almost beyond imagination. As George Buttick remarked at the beginning of the spare age, 'we admire Sputnik and ignore the stars.' It is now our own creation that captures our attention instead. Our animals are anthropomorphized into Mickey Mouse and Snoopy. Tiny transistors are more amazing to us than seeds. Concentrating only on our manufactured things, we have lost the natural world."

Experiencing the Christ of Christmas causes us to step out of the asphalt jungle into the Cathedral of Creation and hear the music of Christmas all around us. "The heavens declare the glory of God; the skies proclaim the work of His hands. Day after day they pour forth speech; night after night they reveal knowledge. There is no speech or language where their voice is not heard. Their voice goes out into all the earth, their words to the ends of the world" (Psalms 19:1-4).

John Michael Talbet says that "everything God has created reveals the divine imprint. The nature of creation manifests the unique signature of the Creator God, just as Picasso's signature in the corner of a painting reveals the work's origin. The harmony evident in our universe is evidence of the divine impetus behind all that exists. The music of creation reveals the interconnectedness of everything that God has made. But beyond that, this cosmic harmony also reveals the unity and melody that exist within the divine nature."

Talbot goes on and points out that, "the music human musicians compose is created for the ears, the emotions, the mind, and the soul. But the music of creation must sink into the deepest realms of our spirit, where it is better understood by intuition than by emotion or thought. Here, working deep within us, this music of creation will bring us into harmony with all of creation, with our human brothers and sister, and with the creator God."

All of creation is praising the Christ of Christmas in Revelation 5.

"Creation waits in eager expectation for the children of God to be revealed."

Romans 8:19

This is because this Christ child as an adult shed His blood in order that sin, which destroys the music and harmony of creation, will be ultimately destroyed. That is why we read in Romans 8:19, "Creation waits in eager expectation for the children of God to be revealed."

Jesus, the Christ of Christmas, is the way, the truth, and the life who reconciles all of creation with God. "God is love" (1 John 4:16) and as His love flows into us through the cleansing power of Jesus Christ it brings harmony and peace into our lives. As this happens it transforms the way we treat the rest of creation to the extent we let the love of the Christ of Christmas flow through us. This changes creation's groaning into creation's music of praise.

"We know that the whole creation has been groaning as in the pains of childbirth right up to the present time. Not only so, but we ourselves, who have the first fruits of the spirit, groan inwardly as we wait eagerly for our adoption to sonship, the redemption of our bodies. For in this hope, we were saved. But hope that is seen is no hope at all. Who hopes for what he already has? But if we hope for what we do not yet have we wait for it patiently" (Romans 8:22-25).

Hearing the music of creation often involves silence, solitude, and stillness. It means leaving the noise of the city behind and going into the solitude of the forest or the park or even the closet. As we do this we let the peace of God create the music of His creation within.

Henri Nouwen in his book, The Way of the Heart, says that "solitude molds self-righteous people into gentle, caring, forgiving persons who are so deeply convinced of their own great sinfulness and so fully aware of God's even greater mercy that their life itself becomes ministry. In such a ministry there is hardly any difference left between doing and being. When we are filled with God's merciful presence, we can do nothing other than minister because our whole being witnesses to the light that has come into

the darkness." Hearing the music of creation and letting it
flow involves first asking God through prayer (Luke 11:9-
13) to give us His Spirit that was present at creation (Genesis 1:2) and at the first Christmas. Second, we surrender
ourselves to God through Jesus Christ and join the rest of
creation in praising God (see Psalms 100, 104). Third, by
faith we expect the creative power of the Spirit to work in
our lives until miraculous signs and wonders follow (Mark
11:22-25). Fourth, we engage in a lifestyle of letting go
of self and surrendering to God. It is then that we let the
music of God's creation flow through us until we are set free
from worry like the birds, flowers, and the rest of creation
(Matthew 6:25-34).

Paul in Philippians 2:6-11 describes how by surrendering
to will of God Jesus let the music of Christmas flow through
Him. "Who, being in very nature God, did not consider
equality with God something to be used to His own advan-
tage; rather, He made himself nothing by taking the very
nature of a servant, being made in human likeness. And
being found in appearance as a man, He humbled Himself
by becoming obedient to death—even death on a cross!
Therefore, God exalted Him to the highest place and gave
Him the name that is above every name, that at the name of
Jesus every knee should bow, in heaven and on earth and
under the earth, and every tongue acknowledge that Jesus
Christ is Lord, to the glory of God the Father."

Look what happened on that first Christmas as the angel
took the music of creation to the men and the animals to
sing the first Christmas Carol, "And there were shepherds
living out in the fields nearby, keeping watch over their
flocks at night. An angel of the Lord appeared to them, and
the glory of the Lord shone around them, and they were terrified. But the angel said to them, "Do not be afraid. I bring
you good news that will cause great joy for all the people.
Today in the town of David a Savior has been born to you;

He is the Messiah, the Lord. This will be a sign to you: You will find a baby wrapped in cloths and lying in a manger. Suddenly a great company of the heavenly host appeared with the angel, praising God and saying, "Glory to God in the highest heaven, and on earth peace to those on whom His favor rests" (Luke 2:8-14).

Jesus is the reason for the music of creation that can be heard not only on Christmas day, but all year long. "The Son is the image of the invisible God, the firstborn over all cre-

ation. For in Him all things were created: things in heaven and on earth, visible and invisible, whether thrones or powers or rulers or authorities; all things have been created through him and for him" (Colossians 1:15-17).

How we need to join in the music of creation and praise God from whom all blessings flow. The problem is that this music is often not heard in our lives because of the struggles of daily living. For that reason, it is critical that we make every effort to not only listen for the music of creation but also participate in it.

There is a shaking going on in the world at this time. Governments are falling. The earth is heating up as climate warming is taking place. Crime is rampant. How we must strive to not let anything keep us from hearing the music of creation and sharing it with others. This means we must not only continue to hear all of creation praising God, but we must join in that praise and worship by letting the love of Christ flow through us into the lives of those in need.

Such love involves the sacrificial love demonstrated through giving. It is this love that John 3:16 speaks of when it says, "God so loved the world He gave His only begotten

Son" (John 3:16). This is the love all of creation is singing about.

The great philosopher Soren Kierkegaard wrote, "The bird on the branch, the Lily in the meadow, the stag in the forest, the fish in the sea, and countless joyful people sing: God is love! But under all these sopranos, as if it were a sustained base part, sounds the de profundi of the sacrifice: God is Love."

Chapter Four- Singing the Songs of Christmas

How I thank God for all the wonderful Christmas music which is like songs in the dark nights of hopelessness and despair. Job cried out for such songs of hope when he declared, "Where is

God my maker, who gives songs in the night" (Job 35:10).

It is because, "God so loved the world that He gave His one and only Son," (John 3:16a) that we can sing the songs of hope on the coldest, loneliest nights that life may throw at us. Not only does God proclaim, "I have loved you with an everlasting love" (Jeremiah 31:3) but He also demonstrated it through sending His Son, Jesus Christ, into the world.

It is this love of God demonstrated through Jesus Christ that the songs of Christmas proclaim Jesus, through His death on the cross. This personally reveals the truth of John 15:13 "Greater love has no one than this, to lay down one's life for one's friends." In Rev. 1:5b-6a we see Jesus described as the One, "Who loves us and has freed us from our sins by

His blood and has made us to be a kingdom of priests to serve His God and Father."

The most published Christmas hymn in North America is Joy to the World. It was written by Isaac Watts, an English minister in 1719.

This Christmas song celebrates not only the birth of Jesus

but His triumphant return. It calls upon humanity to join the rest of creation and celebrate "Joy to the world, the Lord has come, let earth receive her King, let every heart prepare him room."

Charles Spurgeon stated, "Many a night do we have-nights of sorrow, nights of persecution, nights of doubt, nights of bewilderment, nights of anxiety, nights of oppression, nights of ignorance – nights of all kinds, which possess our spirits and terrify our souls. But blessed be God, the Christian can say, 'My God gives me songs in the night."

"Do not be afraid. I bring you good news of great joy that will cause great oy for all the people" Luke 2:10

These songs of hope in the night include that of the angel to the shepherds on that dark night of, "Do not be afraid. I bring you good news of great joy that will cause great joy for all the people" (Luke 2:10).

Why is it so hard for us to receive the Christmas songs of hope in the midst of the nights of disappointment, tragedy, and despair? These songs of hope are actually the proclamation of God's love revealed through the scripture, the millions of forms of art called creation and the presence of the Holy Spirit. That same Spirit of God, which from the beginning of time hovers over the waters of emptiness, formlessness and darkness, desires to bring forth order and light (see Genesis 1:1-4) in our lives.

We are told explicitly in Romans 8:38-39 that nothing can separate us from the love of God which we celebrate at Christmas. "No, in all these things we are more than conquerors through Him who loved us. For I am convinced that neither death nor life, neither angels nor demons, neither the present nor the future, nor any powers, neither height nor depth, nor anything else in all creation, will be able to separate us from the love of God that is in Christ Jesus our Lord."

The words for one of the most popular Christmas songs, "Hark! The Herald Angels Sing" was written by John Wesley in 1739. The purpose of the song was to show Christ's intention to not only redeem humanity but all of creation. This is heard in the words, "Peace on earth and mercy mild, God and sinners reconciled" in verse one, and "Light and life to all He brings, Risen with healing in His wings" in verse 3.

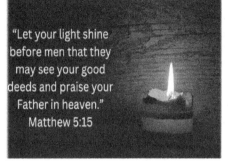

"Let your light shine before men that they may see your good deeds and praise your Father in heaven."
Matthew 5:15

These songs of God's love which flow through the scriptures and the wonders of creation are personified through the Risen Christ. They are the gifts that keep on giving. Not only are we to be the recipients of such gifts, but we are to also freely share that which we have been given. In Matt. 5:15 Jesus commands us to, "Let your light (of love) shine before men (and women) that they may see your good deeds and praise your Father in heaven."

As believers it is necessary that we not only listen to the Christmas songs of love and hope that God shares with us in the darkness of life but also that we share them with others who are going through difficult times. Jesus declares, "I tell you, whatever you did for one of the least of these brothers and sisters of Mine, you did for Me" (Matt. 25:40).

Sing out my friend in word and deed the Christmas songs of hope, help and direct love that are so desperately needed in the darkness of this age in which we live. God has chosen you for this time and place in history.

"O Come Let Us Adore Him Christ the Lord." We adore Him because, "Heaven came down and glory filled my soul. When at the cross, my Savior made me whole. My sins were washed away, and my night was turned to day... Now I have the hope that will surely endure.

It is because of the Christ of Christmas we can sing out in the midst of a world of darkness. "Yet this I call to mind and therefore I have hope" (Lamentations 3:21). There is nothing like singing to keep your spirit alive. It will also encourage others around you who would otherwise be adversely affected by your negative attitude. Remember, as you keep your mouth full of songs, you will keep your heart full of praise as you put your hands to work helping others who are going through the dark valley of trouble.

As we sing the songs of Christmas, we will see the door between heaven and earth until we feel like we are singing with the angels as they sang to the shepherds of the birth of our Immanuel.

Mary after hearing from the angel she was to bring forth the Christ child, burst forth with, "My soul glorifies the Lord, and my spirit rejoices in God my Savior.... He has brought down rulers from their thrones but has lifted up the humble. He has filled the hungry with good things but has sent the rich away empty" (Luke 1:46, 52, 53).

The angels witnessing the promise and the prophesies fulfilled through the birth of Christ praised God declaring

"Glory to God in the highest heaven, and on earth peace to those on whom His favor rests."

Oh, what a Holy Night it is as we sing with the angels who declared, "We bring you good tidings of great joy for unto you is born this day in the City of David, a Savior, who is Christ the Lord."

Now may the songs of Christmas fill your mind and spirit until the darkness of the nights of despair and loneliness are gone.

Chapter 5: The Miracle of Love

The miracle of Christmas is one where the creator and designer of the universe sends His Son to be born as a homeless baby in a world intoxicated by anger, greed, and fear.

I cannot recall a Christmas season where there has been so much anger, bitterness, and hatred. I know if I join the multitudes who blame the president, the internet, the media, and even the church, I won't have a blessed Christmas. The blame game may leave me momentarily satisfied in my comfort zone, but in the long run, I will be the big loser when it comes to getting a clearer understanding of the real meaning of Christmas.

I have come to the realization that if Christmas is going to have any meaning this year, I must leave this zone of bitterness and enter the world of faith and love that the presence of Christ provides.

The angel declared this on that first Christmas with the words, "Do not be afraid. I bring you good news that will cause great joy for all people. Today, in the town of David a Savior, has been born to you; he is the Messiah, the Lord" (Luke 2:10-11).

It would be so much easier to do what so many Christmas cards do. This happens when the baby, the angels, and shepherds are all presented as just another story in a different time and place. But this year, I can't do that and hope to get any real meaning out of Christmas.

I know that this Christmas I need the miracle of God's love more than ever before. It is this realization that causes the inner struggle to begin. It is so much easier to build walls and only associate with people who agree with my point of view. What is needed this Christmas are bridges to others I differ with to understand their fears and concerns.

It is this miracle of Christmas that God is with us that awakens the realizations that those we differ with are fellow human beings that are made in the image of God, and He also loves each and every one of them.

Now as I pray that there might be peace on earth and that God's revolution of love would take place, I must let it begin with me. Unless I face the bitterness and unloving attitudes in my own life, I will never really be free to spread that love.

Thank God for the Miracle of Christmas where God's perfect love casts out all fear and bitterness. This allows me to see those I differ from as fellow human beings with their own struggles and fears. As I do this, I know I will be opening the door to a deeper understanding of the miracle of love than I have ever had before.

The Miracle of Love is all about engagement. It involves God engaging with humanity by sending His Son into the world. Jesus came with compassion, getting His hands dirty,

 sore, and worn in service with the promise that He has come to set the captives free. Jesus provided this freedom through His death on the cross for our sins and His conquering of death through His resurrection.

If we are not careful it is so easy to lose sight of this true meaning of Christmas. Each year, stores are starting earlier and earlier to entice people to buy things for Christmas. Buying more possessions becomes the central focus of

Christmas. For many in America, possessions can easily come to possess. This materialistic system views individuals as consumers and markets to be exploited.

At this point, you may be saying, "What does this have to do with me? I don't have possessions to be possessed with." Matthew 6:21 says, "For where your treasure is, there your heart will be also." The question for you and me this Christmas is where is my heart? What really is the most important thing to me?

Jesus tells us in Matthew 23:37-40, "Love the Lord your God with all your heart and with all your soul and with all your mind. This is the first and greatest commandment. And the second is like it; Love your neighbor as yourself. All the law and prophets hang on these two commands."

When we experience the truth of this in the depth of our being, we have come to learn the real meaning of Christmas. Such an experience provides a freedom that Paul expresses in Philippians 4:12-13, "I know what it is to be in need, and I know what it is to have plenty. I have learned the secret of being content in any and every situation, whether well fed or hungry, whether living in plenty or in want. I can do all this through Him who gives me strength."

It is this miracle of Christmas in us, which provides the freedom for us to give up our possession to those in need rather than be possessed by them. This freedom to give, in realization that all we have has been freely given to us by God, is that secret that Paul learned when it came to being content in whatever the circumstances may be (Philippians 4:11). As he continues to outline the blessings of giving in Philippians 4:11-19, he states in verse 17, "Not that I desire your gifts, what I desire is that more be credited to your account."

Jesus explains this further when He says in Matthew 6:19-21, "Do not store up for yourselves treasures on earth, where moth and rust destroy, and where thieves break in and steal. But store up for yourselves treasures in heaven, where moth and rust do not destroy and where thieves do not break in and steal. For where your treasure is, there your heart will be also." The fact is that none of earth's posses-sions or treasures come anywhere close to giving

Where is your Treasure?

that sense of fulfillment that comes through helping some-one in need throughout the love of Jesus Christ.

We are free to share with those in need because we know that Jesus Christ is with us. Jesus, who was fully God and man is called in Matthew 1:23, "Immanuel...God with us." C.S. Lewis writes, "In the Christmas story, God descends to re-ascend. He comes down from the heights of absolute be-ing into time and space, down into humanity; down further still, if embryologists are right, to recapitulate in the womb of ancient and pre-human phases of life; down to the very roots and seabed of the Nature He has created."

It is the fulfillment of this promise of God coming among us through Christ that we celebrate at Christmas. This Christmas gift is commonly referred to as good news or the gospel. Jim Wallis in his book, "Agenda for Biblical People" explains that "The gospel calls for radical allegiance to a Kingdom that is at fundamental variance with the 'prin-cipalities and powers' which rules the world system. The standards and values of the world undergo a trans-valua-tion, a reversal, an inversion in Jesus Christ. A commitment to Christ entails a radical change in our relationship to money and possessions, violence and war, power status, success, leadership, ideology, and the state. Our relationship to Christ gives us a new relationship to the persons and especially to the poor, the weak, the broken, the outcasts, the "enemies" and the victims of the various systems of the world."

Jesus' proclamation of freedom is good news to everyone who is captivated by this world's materialistic system. He offers healing to those who have been blinded by their possessions, as well as to those who have been stepped on and kicked aside because they are poor or homeless.

In Luke 4:18-19, Jesus declared, "The Spirit of the Lord is on me because He anointed me to proclaim good news to the poor. He has sent me to proclaim freedom for the prisoners, and recovery of sight for the blind, to set the oppressed free, to proclaim the year of the Lord's favor."

Ron Sider in his book, *Genuine Christianity*, states, "Blatant disobedient conformity to the world has plagued Christians for centuries. We have launched vicious crusades to slaughter Muslims; we have fabricated "biblical" arguments to justify slavery and racism. Now, as the modern world redefines happiness as individual self-fulfillment and ever expanding, material abundance, we construct new gospels of wealth and self-esteem. The world sneers at our hypocrisy, convinced that Christians, who largely defy the One they allegedly worship, have nothing to offer."

"At one time, Mahatma Gandhi, the greatest Hindu of the twentieth century, seriously considered accepting the claims of Christ because he loved the Jesus of the Gospels. But when he compared how Christians live with the teachings of Jesus, Gandhi turned away in revulsion. He said,

"I consider Western Christianity in its practical working a negation of Christ's Christianity."

"Thank God that is not the whole story. Even at the worst of times, a faithful remnant has dared to challenge the status quo by living like Jesus."

Challenging the status quo involves confronting the hatred, bitterness, and greed in our world with the love of Jesus Christ that dwells within us. This means we must let Jesus be Lord of our lives. As Lord of our lives, the Miracle of Christmas will then be free to work in us as we do what Jesus tells us to do in Matthew 5:16. "Let your light shine before others, that they may see your good works and glorify your Father in Heaven" (Matthew 5:16).

Chapter Six: The Journey

Christmas is a journey from the beginning of earth's existence and continues into eternity. This journey starts in Genesis 3:15 with the declaration that the coming Messiah will crush the head of Satan. It continues through the covenants made with Abraham and David.

Over three hundred prophecies are given throughout the Old Testament concerning the Messiah. These prophecies ranged from where Christ the Messiah would be born (Micah 5:24) to how He would be rejected and crucified (Psalm 22:16-17).

The journey of the coming of the Messiah is one woven throughout the Old Testament. Both Matthew and Luke show with their detailed chronologies the ancestry of the Messiah, Jesus Christ. Luke traces how the ancestry of Jesus goes all the way back to Adam.

Matthew's journey through Jesus' past takes us back to Abraham. Matthew's genealogy is unlike other Jewish genealogies in that it includes women. These four women include Tamar, who was involved in a scandal with Judah (Genesis 38); Rahab, the Canaanite prostitute who was from Jericho (Joshua 2); Ruth the Moabite along with Bathsheba who was involved in an adulterous relationship with David. Matthew shows us from this chronology how God's grace can take the lowest on the cultural ladder and then place them in the royal lineage.

The initial journey's completion of divinity inhabiting humanity, required a series of historical occurrences to make the proclamation of the Divine Act a success. It included the conquests of Alexander the Great which resulted in the language of Greek being spread throughout the then known world.

Next came the world domination by Rome. This spread the second language of Latin and created a road system surpassing all that had existed in the past. These historical developments are important because once the arrival of the Messiah takes place, its proclamation can spread like wild-fire through a dry dead forest.

When the time had come for the story of the Messiah's arrival to be told it was done on a dark night, outside of Bethlehem. The declaration was made to a group of Shepherds who were watching their flock of sheep. Suddenly the sky lit up with the glory of God. Then an angel told the Shepherds, "Do not be afraid. I bring you good news that will cause great joy for all the people. Today in the town of David a Savior has been born to you; He is the Messiah, the Lord. This will be a sign to you: you will find a baby wrapped in cloths and lying in a manger. Suddenly a great company of the heavenly host appeared with the angel, praising God and saying, 'Glory to God in the highest heaven, and on earth peace to those on whom His favor rests'" (Luke 2:10-15).

Upon hearing the broadcast by the heavenly host, the Shepherds then immediately went to Bethlehem to look for the child.

Upon arriving there they found a newly born houseless child that had been placed in a manger. After the shepherds left, the Christ child was presented in the temple. At this dedication both Simeon and Anna, who were in attendance, recognized Him as the promised Messiah. Simeon declares, "For my eyes have seen your salva-tion, which you have prepared in the sight of all nations:

a light for revelation to the Gentiles, and the glory of your people Israel (Luke 2:30-32).

The light for the revelation to the Gentiles came to the Magi, or the wise men, in the form of a star. When they stopped and asked King Herod, "Where is the King of the Jews?" Herod immediately asked the wise men to return and tell him where the child was at. He wanted to kill this threat to his throne.

The journey for the wise men were completed as they followed the star to the Christ child's crib. There they left gold, frankincense, and myrrh, not realizing that their gift of love would help finance the Holy families escape from the murderous hand of Herod.

When the wise men did not return to Herod and tell him where the child resided, the demon possessed, power hungry Herod then ordered the killing of every boy in Bethlehem who was two years and younger. This act of violence did not take place until Joseph had been warned by an angel in a dream to flee with Mary and the baby to Egypt. There they resided as refugees until Herod died, after which they returned to Nazareth. This further fulfilled that which was spoken by the prophets.

The journey of Messiah had just begun. It continues to unfold as Jesus becomes an adult. When he was approximately 30 years of age, John baptized Jesus. As John did this, the Holy Spirit, in the form of a dove landed upon Christ  the Messiah and the voice of God the Father declared, "This is my son whom I love; with Him I am well pleased" (Luke 3:22).

After the dynamic Baptism experience, "Jesus was led by

the spirit into the wilderness to be tempted by the devil" (Matthew 4:1).

After fasting forty days and forty nights Jesus was famished. It was then Satan attacked with three temptations to get Jesus to take a different journey than that of the cross. These temptations were for Christ to use His powers to meet His own needs, by turning stones into bread. Then, Satan tempts Jesus to jump off the highest point of the temple. Such a jump would create a scene that would bring Jesus' notoriety and the ability to avoid the cross. Finally, Satan says worship me and you can have it all. Each time Jesus uses the sharp two-edged sword of the Word of God to resist the devil until finally Jesus declares, "Away from me, Satan! For it is written: 'Worship the Lord your God and serve Him only" (Matthew 4:10).

The devil then leaves Jesus and He continues His three-year journey to the cross. As He journeys, Jesus heals the sick, raises the dead, casts out demons and declares the Kingdom of God has arrived. Jesus, with each step of His journey, gets closer to fulfilling His mission to save humanity.

The purpose of Christ's journey on earth was to die on a cross for the sins of humanity. It was a journey to restore a creation that had been contaminated by sin.

Satan would not give up. Where before he tried using Herod and then tempting Jesus, now Satan was going to turn his demons loose on the religious leaders and a disciple called Judas.

Jesus, on the day we know as Palm Sunday, fulfilled Zachariah's prophecy of Zechariah 9:9 where it says, "Rejoice greatly, Daughter

Zion! Shout, Daughter Jerusalem! See your king comes to you, righteous and victorious, lowly, and riding on a donkey, on a colt, the foal of a donkey."

As the citizens of Jerusalem shouted their hosannas the enemy was at work. Satan was busy stirring up the greed and the self-serving ambition in Judas. He knew Judas had seen Jesus' miracles during the past three years. So, Satan convinced Judas, that if he turned Jesus over to the religious and political authorities, Jesus would use his miraculous powers to destroy the Romans and set up His kingdom on earth.

The stage was set. Judas betrayed Jesus with a kiss. The problem for Judas was that from that moment on, everything as far as Judas planned went wrong. Instead of wiping out those who seized Him, Jesus healed the one whose ear Peter had cut off. Then, Jesus surrendered to the authorities. After this happened, Judas, in despair, went out and hung himself.

Even though Judas hung himself, Satan was delighted. With each twist and turn in the journey to the cross Satan danced with triumph. He knew the Messiah was about to die.

Satan felt his moment of victory had arrived. Jesus, the Messiah, the Savior of humanity was nailed to the cross.

Satan rejoiced because he believed he had wiped out God's plan for redemption. The anointed one, the Savior of the world, was dead. Suddenly as Satan and his demons were celebrating there was a knock at the door of hell. When they opened it, they came face to face with the crucified Christ.

Peter described this event in I Peter 3:18-19, "For Christ also suffered once for sins, the righteous for the unrighteous, to bring you to God. He was put to death in the body but made alive in the Spirit. After being made alive, he went and made proclamation to the imprisoned spirits."

These imprisoned spirits in hell were liberated and all hell broke loose. As this happened, on earth the curtain in the temple ripped in two, and many who were dead arose and walked the streets of Jerusalem. All this was a preview of what was to happen on that glorious resurrection day.

On the third day as the sun rose, the stone in front of the tomb blew out like a cork on a bottle. Christ then came out of the grave triumphantly. He had defeated sin, death, and the devil.

Even with this victorious resurrection the journey was still not completed. Jesus returned triumphantly to heaven but before leaving He promised to send His comforter, the Holy Spirit, to those who remained on earth traveling their individual spiritual journeys.

The bride of Christ which includes each of us believers, will on the completion of our journey here on Earth, be united with our bride groom, the Risen Savior, Jesus Christ. He is the beginning and the end of the journey. The Alpha and Omega. Oh, what a wonderful day that will be!

Let's look at what is waiting for us when we complete our journey on earth and join Christ in heaven. "Then I heard what sounded like a great multitude, like the roar of rushing waters and like loud peals of thunder, shouting: 'Hallelujah! For our Lord God Almighty reigns. Let us rejoice and be glad and give him glory! For the wedding of the Lamb has come, and his bride has made herself ready" (Revelation 19:6).

Chapter Seven: Christmas Freedom

Christmas is all about engagement. It involves God engaging with humanity by sending Jesus, His Son into the world. Jesus came with  compassion, getting His hands dirty, sore, and worn in service with the promise that He has come to set the captives free. He provided this freedom through His death on the cross for our sins. Then He conquered death through His resurrection. This is the true meaning of Christmas.

Many have forgotten this as stores start earlier and earlier to entice people to buy things for Christmas. Buying more possessions then becomes the central focus of Christmas. This materialistic system views individuals as consumers and markets to be exploited.

 Matthew 6:21 says, "For where your treasure is, there your heart will be also." The question for you and me is, where is my heart? What really is the most important thing to me? Jesus says in Matthew 22:37-40, "Love the Lord your God with all your heart and with all your soul and with all your mind. This is the first and greatest commandment. And the

second is like it; Love your neighbor as yourself. All the law and prophets hang on these two commandments."

When one experiences the truth of this in the depth of their being they have come to learn the real meaning of Christmas. Such an experience provides a freedom that Paul expresses in Philippians 4:12-13, "I know what it is to be in need, and I know what it is to have plenty. I have learned the secret of being content in any and every situation, whether well fed or hungry, whether living in plenty or in want. I can do everything through Him who gives me strength."

It is this miracle of Christmas which provides the freedom for us to give up our possessions to those in need rather than be possessed by them. This freedom to give, is that secret that Paul learned when it came to being content in whatever the circumstances may be (Philippians 4:11). As he continues to outline the blessings of giving in Philippians 4:11-19, he states in verse 17, "Not that I desire your gifts; what I desire is that more be credited to your account."

Jesus explains this further when he says in Matthew 6:19-21, "Do not store up for yourselves treasures on earth, where moths and vermin destroy, and where thieves break in and steal. But store up for yourselves treasures in heaven, where moth and rust do not destroy and where thieves do not break in and steal. For where your treasure is, there your heart will be also."

How we need to thank God for sharing the treasure of His Son, Jesus Christ with us. Jesus was born into the world as a baby to set the captives free. Christmas Freedom is the fulfillment of the promise of God coming among us through the Christ that we celebrate at Christmas. This Christmas gift of Freedom from sin, death, and the devil is commonly referred to as good news or the gospel.

Jesus' proclamation of freedom is good news to everyone

who is poor or captivated by this world's materialistic system. He offers healing to those who have been blinded by their possessions as well as freedom to the ones who have been stepped on and kicked aside because they are poor or homeless.

In Luke 4:18, 19 Jesus defined his mission by declaring, "The Spirit of the Lord is upon me, because He anointed me to proclaim good news to the poor. He has sent me to proclaim freedom for the prisoners and recovery of sight for the blind, to set the oppressed free, to proclaim the year of the Lord's favor."

Colossians 1:15-17 explains who Jesus is and why He can make such a proclamation. "The Son is the image of the invisible God, the firstborn over all creation. For in Him all things were created: things in heaven and on earth, visible and invisible, whether thrones or powers or rulers or authorities; all things have been created through Him and for Him. He is before all things, and in Him all things hold together."

The time has come to let the Christ of Christmas set us free. In these verses we see the word all used five times. We discover Christ the creator who is the "firstborn over all creation, for by Him all things were created." We also discover that the Christ of Christmas is  the sustainer as well as the creator and that "all things were created by Him and for Him. He is before all things, and in Him all things hold together."

As we continue to look at Colossians 1:18-20 we see that the Christ of Christmas is not only creator and sustainer, but also ruler, reconciler, and redeemer. "And He is the head of the body, the church; He is the beginning and the firstborn from among the dead, so that in everything He might have the supremacy. For God was pleased to have all His fullness dwell in Him, and through Him to reconcile to Himself all things, whether things on earth or things in heaven, by making peace through His blood shed on the cross."

Jesus as the Christ of Christmas, who is our creator, sustainer, ruler, reconciler, and redeemer has come to set us free. In Him we can find a peace, a power, and a purpose that all the possessions of this world could never give us.

Jonathan Edwards, experiencing a great spiritual awakening, believed that God made it possible for humans through Jesus Christ to be recreated in God's image. As a result, we are able to engage deeply and inwardly with God through Christ and the beauty of His creation. Edwards stated, "God's excellency, His wisdom, His purity and love, seemed to appear in everything, in the sun, moon and stars: in the clouds and blue sky; in the grass, flowers, trees, in the water, and all nature."

Because God reveals Himself through the Bible and His creation, we must speak up when we hear that a species is destroyed every 8 hours. We cannot be indifferent as the earth's oxygen is rapidly being depleted by the felling of 25 million acres of rain forestry each year, and carbon dioxide is being pumped into the air at record rates.

Ron Sider in his book, *Genuine Christianity*, explains how true believers are different from those who commonly refer to themselves as Christians. He writes, "most Christians mimic the world! They are often as self-centered, as sexually promiscuous, as racist, and materialistic as their unbelieving friends. They worship wealth, commit adultery, file for divorce, and destroy the environ-

ment like their neighbors."

Sider continues, "Thank God that is not the whole story. Even at the worst of times, a faithful remnant has dared to challenge the status quo by living like Jesus."

A redeemed people are a liberated people, set free from the destructive power of sin with its addiction to things. Such sin drives greed, self-centeredness, and self-serving attitudes, which contribute directly and indirectly to the destruction of the earth and the oppression of the poor. That's why we read in Romans 8:19-21, "For the creation waits in eager expectation for the children of God to be revealed. For the creation was subjected to frustration, not by its own choice, but by the will of the one who subjected it, in hope that the creation itself will be liberated from its bondage to decay and brought into the freedom and glory of the children of God."

Those experiencing this glorious freedom will be able to protect creation as they freely share with the hurting and the homeless. The liberated will experience the freedom to enjoy giving as their hearts and minds are open to all that God has given. They will rejoice in the wonders of creation and the coming of Christ to the extent they can declare along with the Psalmist in Psalm 8:13, "Lord, our Lord, how majestic is your name in all the earth! You

have set your glory in the heavens... When I consider your heavens, the work of your fingers, the moon and the stars, which you have set in place."

Those who have experienced the freedom of Christmas are no longer possessed by their possessions. They have been set free to worship Christ as they work to preserve all of creation realizing it does not exist for mankind but for the creator. They are a people who have been redeemed to live for His glory, which dictates they are an involved people. Those who have been set free by the Christ of Christmas will work to preserve all of life including the poor, the fatherless, the hurting and the homeless.

Jesus has come to give life! He died and rose to set us free from the hopelessness and despair that being possessed by possessions brings. Remember, Jesus is the Reason for the Season. Let us live and share that hope in all we do and say.

Chapter Eight: Overcoming Fear through the Miracle of Christmas

Fear is mounting worldwide with the increased numbers of wars as well as one natural disaster after another takes place. Presently, we are watching the words of Jesus found in Luke 21:25-26 being fulfilled before us; "... On the earth, nations will be in anguish and perplexity... People will faint from terror, apprehensive of what is coming on the world, for the heavenly bodies will be shaken."

For the followers of Jesus there is a freedom of fear that passes all understanding. This freedom comes from surrendering ourselves by faith, into the care of God. It means putting ourselves completely under His wisdom, power, and provision. If we do this, the God of heaven and earth promises to be totally responsible for our daily provision because He is a God of Love.

This reality was driven home to me when I visited Rob and Judy who direct the By His Grace Food Pantry in Sutherland Springs, Texas. This outreach is run by the First Baptist Church. This is the church where the largest mass murder that had ever taken place in a sanctuary had happened twelve days before my visit.

The previous director of the food pantry was Lula White. She was one of the 26 who had been killed in the church on Sunday, November 5, 2017, while 20 others were wounded.

Lula White

It became clear as I talked to Rob and Judy, that they, along with other members of the congregation who remained alive, were determined to continue to serve the Lord as they found security in His love.

For one to experience the certainty of this love of God they must believe the words that the Angel spoke to the shepherds in Luke 2:10-11. "Do not be afraid. I bring you good news that will cause great joy for all the people. Today in the town of David a Savior has been born to you; He is the Messiah, the Lord."

Personally accepting this good news makes it possible for Christmas to become one of the brightest times of the year. When we respond like Mary did in Luke 1:38, "May your word to me be fulfilled," we give God permission to let the love He showed at that First Christmas take place in our lives.

The reason we often miss the miracle of Christmas is because misguided materialism drives us into such a frenzied pace that it turns the miracle of Christmas into a time of fear, depression, and frustration.

I was reminded by my new friends in Sutherland Springs that "There is no fear in love. But perfect love drives out fear" (1 John 4:18).

If we believe that we are loved by God, we will experience the powerful antidote to the poison of fear. God demonstrated that love by sending His Son into the world. That is the good news we read about in John 3:16 that, "For God so loved the world that He gave His one and only Son, that whoever believes in Him shall not perish but have eternal life." This Christmas gift described in John 3:16 frees us to live a life that is not paralyzed by fear.

Pastor Frank Pomeroy and his wife Sherri had been out of town on that Sunday when tragedy struck at Sutherland Springs Baptist Church. The following Sunday under a large tent he declared to a record number of people attending the service, "Rather than choose the darkness that the young man did that day, we choose life." Frank and Sherri's 14-year-old daughter, Annabelle, were among those killed in the November 5th rampage. Frank shared, "I know everyone who gave their life that day. Some of whom were my best friends and my daughter. I guarantee they are dancing with Jesus today."

No matter what life may bring, this Christmas, we can celebrate the life, death, and resurrection of Jesus Christ. The fact is He died for our sins, and now we can dance with Jesus for all eternity. Those who don't feel like dancing with Jesus need to re-read the Christmas Story which is filled with one, "fear not" after another.

The angel said to Mary, "Do not be afraid, Mary... The Holy Spirit will come on you, and the power of the Most High will overshadow you... For no word from God will ever fail" (Luke 1:30, 35, 37).

As we struggle with God's promise and plans for us, we need to let His "fear not" reassure us that His power and provision is sufficient to meet every need. In Luke 2:10-11 we see the angel telling the shepherds, "Do not be afraid. I bring you good news that will cause great joy for all the people. Today in the town of David a Savior has been born to you; He is the Messiah, the Lord."

Just as the shepherds were told, even so we must also be reminded that in spite of the circumstances, miracles are often born in the least expected times and places! Joseph was reminded of this when the angel told him, "Joseph son of David, do not be afraid to take Mary home as your wife, because what is conceived in her is from the Holy Spirit" (Matthew 1:20).

Like Joseph, we also must be reminded that faith means loving someone enough to not judge him or her or cast them aside. Instead, we need to trust that God is at work in that person's life. Joseph, instead of walking out on the relationship, believed God's promise and stuck with it despite the circumstances.

Rob, Judy, Pastor Frank, and Sherri did not let the murder of their church family stop them. Sherri said, "Our church was not comprised of members or parishioners. We were a very close family. We ate together, we laughed together, we cried together, and we worshipped together."

As I toured that church sanctuary, I saw 26 white chairs with a rose along with a cross and the name of the person killed there painted on each chair. As I observed this, I knew I was in the presence of the Lord.

The words of those killed and wounded, which was recorded at previous services played in the background. Each testified of their faith and reminded me of the need to trust the Christ of Christmas each and every day of the year.

Jesus declares, "Very truly I tell you, whoever believes in me will do the works I have been doing, and they will do even greater things than these, because I am going to the Father. And I will do whatever you ask in my name, so that the Father may be glorified in the Son. You may ask me for anything in my name, and I will do it" (John 14:12-14).

With a promise like that, we have no excuse for letting fear dominate our lives. But that is not all; Jesus has given us the "Spirit of Truth," the Holy Spirit and "He lives with you and will be in you" (John 14:17).

Jesus goes on to promise, "But the Advocate, the Holy Spirit, whom the Father will send in my name, will teach you all things and will remind you of everything I have said to you" (John 14:26).

Now in the name of Jesus, we must let fear be gone as we let the Holy Spirit work in our lives. For Jesus says, "Peace I leave with you; My peace I give you. I do not give to you as the world gives. Do not let your hearts be troubled and do not be afraid" (John 14:27).

This peace is possible if we, as branches remain in Jesus, the vine. Jesus declares in John 15:5, "I am the vine; you are the branches. If you remain in Me and I in you, you will bear much fruit; apart from Me you can do nothing."

Rob and Judy believed these words of Jesus. For some reason they could not explain why they had come to church late that Sunday morning of November 5th. When they arrived at church, the wounded were being brought out of the church by first responders. It was then they knew God had kept them alive for a purpose.

I saw that purpose being lived out as Rob and Judy ministered to those who had come for food at the pantry. This pantry was located in a house next to the church. Many of the poor and elderly people who received food expressed their grief over the death of Lula White, the previous food pantry director, and others who had been killed.

Earlier that day as my son Chris and I traveled to Sutherland Springs I had voiced my frustration over how New Life Evangelistic Center had been driven out of our church building at 1411 Locust. Now in my final conversation with Rob I felt the Holy Spirit wanted to drive home to me how important it was that I also remained true to the mission God had given me. I found myself saying to Rob, "We both have been driven out of our church buildings. You and your congregation by a mad man who shot over half the congregation. We have been driven out by wealthy condominium owners who don't want our homeless church members in the neighborhood. But we can't give up. The church is bigger than a building. We will continue despite what the devil might throw at us as I John 4:4 tells us, "You, dear children, are from God and have overcome them, because the one who is in you is greater than the one who is in the world."

Rob and Judy readily agreed and continued to share with me the miracles they were seeing take place.

As they shared, Deuteronomy 20:3-4 came to mind where it says, "Do not be fainthearted or afraid; do not panic or be terrified by them. For the Lord your God is the one who goes with you to fight for you against your enemies to give you victory."

We are told in Hebrews 2:14b- that, "Through death He might destroy the one who has the power of death, that is, the devil, and deliver all those who through fear of death were subject to lifelong slavery."

Liberated from a fear of death, through the death and resurrection of Jesus Christ, we are now free, like Rob and Judy, to reach out to those in need. Deuteronomy 24:10-22, and Deuteronomy 27: 19 show God's great concern for the needy.

In Deuteronomy 28 we see what blessings await those who obey the Lord. In that same chapter we also read what happens to those who disobey. It is fear, which often paralyzes and keeps individuals from reaching out to the poor and homeless. If we are going to be truly effective in the work of God, we must let Him lift us above our fears, freeing us to be there when people are hurting.

If we are going to overcome fear this Christmas we must let every Christmas light that we see remind us that, "God is light, pure light; there's not a trace of darkness in Him.

If we claim that we experience a shared life with Him and continue to stumble around in the dark, we're obviously lying through our teeth—we're not living what we claim. But if we walk in the light, God Himself being the light, we also experience a shared life with one another, as the sacrificed blood of Jesus, God's Son, purges all our sins" (1 John 1:5-7, The Message Bible).

At first Zacharias did not accept the light the angel was sharing with him. As a result of his doubting, he was not able to speak until the angel's words were fulfilled in their own time (Luke 1:20). Even though his faith was slow, he remained faithful. After he held his newborn son in his own two hands, he was able to speak and he  declared, "his name is John", then Zacharias offered a song of praise to God (See Luke 1:57-80). The last part of this song of praise goes like this, "Through the heartfelt mercies of our God, God's Sunrise will break in upon us, shining on those in the darkness, those sitting in the shadow of death. Then showing us the way, one foot at a time, down the path of peace" (Luke 1:79b The Message Bible).

No matter what we have been through this year we must allow the miracles of Christmas to work in our lives. Let us believe and fear not, knowing that the wonder of Christmas is upon us. Christ has come, and it is His light that has driven the darkness of fear from our lives. Because of His death and resurrection, we can be set free from the slavery of sin

Christmas is the celebration of more than a baby in a manger. It is the celebration of the new life and freedom that Christ provides both now and for all eternity.

Chapter Nine - Home for Christmas

There is something about being home for Christmas that stirs up the childhood dreams of Christmas. Dreams that Bing Crosby sang about, "I'll be home for Christmas, if only in my dreams."

You may be one of those who don't have a home, or you may be separated from family and friends. You feel like a cosmic orphan set adrift in a hostile universe. For some, home is a shack with frozen water pipes, no heat, or lights. If you are experiencing such difficulties, you are not alone. Christmas is the story of a road weary homeless couple who found themselves in a stable among animals because there was no room for them in the inn.

The houseless know what it is like, to be locked out, unable to find an apartment because of the lack of employment as developers receive tax abatements, CDA grants and the power of eminent domain. If you find yourself locked

out in the stable, realize you may be penniless, but you are not powerless. You may feel hopeless, but you are not helpless. Rise Up – turn to the source of absolute power – The Christ of Christmas.

Come home to Him now and discover there is a light that is not only shining over you but desires to shine in you. Jesus is the light of the world, who died and rose to give all of us, rich or poor, life both now and for all eternity. I come to you right now as one who can testify from personal experience that it is the living Jesus who has given me the strength to go year after year finding a home in the presence of the Heavenly Father.

I have learned that God's plan for my life involves supernatural seasons. I am reminded of this with the evergreen Christmas tree in the cold winter months when most of the other trees have lost their leaves. In spite of the circumstances, I can also remain alive as I move forward with a certain rhythm of heavenly timing. I have seen that as I pass through winter, spring, summer and fall that God has everything under control. "There is a time for everything, and a season for every activity under the heavens" (Ecclesiastes 3:1).

The Story of Christmas teaches me that I need to look for God's perfect timing and recognize when it comes. Jesus corrected those who noticed only the seasons but ignored the signs of the times of what God was doing in the world and in their personal lives (Matthew 16:3). How I need to seek God during this Christmas season to discover His power of supernatural seasons in my life.

Tragically many this Christmas season, even though they have homes, feel hopeless and homeless. They have lost the true meaning of Christmas among the neon lights, the commercialism, and the Christmas parades which promote everything from Bugs Bunny to Santa Claus but ignore the Christ of Christmas. So many have forgotten that the true meaning of Christmas is the Celebration of the birth of Christ. We must remember, God entrusted His only son not to Herod or to city hall, the state capitol, or the Roman government, but to a homeless couple.

Mary and Joseph had submitted themselves to Caesars' census, but when they got to Bethlehem, they discovered that Herod's friends had all the rooms in the Inn. But Mary and Joseph didn't crash under the pressure of the bureaucracy. They turned to God. Sure, they ended up in a stable. Yes, Mary could have died in childbirth, and indeed Jesus was swaddled in rags because His mother – like so many of the homeless mothers had neither diapers or pampers, But God had everything predestined and under control.

Mary and Joseph probably were not aware that above them, beyond the darkness and hopelessness of their situation, a beautiful bright star was shining. That star was not going unnoticed.

Three wise men saw the star and they decided to respond. They went to the homeless child where a star was shining over conditions that some could have found depressing.

The miracle of Christmas involves the miracle of the incarnation where Jesus was conceived through the power of the Holy Spirit without the involvement of a human father (Luke 1:35). This made it possible for God, the Son, to become a human being without giving up His deity.

When we accept the reality of this miracle, we are then able to realize that the celebration of Christmas is the celebration of God's miracle power. This realization allows us to come home to Him in a new and powerful way. This means that when things look impossible, we are reminded that Jesus is the living miracle. "With man this is impossible, but with God all things are possible" (Matthew 19:26).

When we try to be at home with Jesus, we often find ourselves frequently facing opposition, doubt, and fear. God's response throughout the Christmas Story is "fear not." The angel said to Mary, "Fear not, Mary... The Holy Ghost will come upon you, and the power of the Highest shall overshadow you. . . For no word from God will ever fail" (Luke 1:30, 35, 37).

As we struggle with God's promise and plans for us, we need to let His "fear not" reassure us that His power and provision are sufficient to meet every need. In Luke 2:10-11 we see the angel telling the shepherds, "Do not be afraid. I bring you good news that will cause great joy for all the people. Today in the town of David a Savior has been born to you; he is the Messiah, the Lord."

Just as the shepherds were told, even so we must also be reminded that in spite of the circumstances, miracles are often born in the least expected times and places!

Joseph is another example of one who was told not to fear. "Joseph, son of David, do not be afraid to take Mary home as your wife, because what is conceived in her is from the Holy Spirit" (Matthew 1:20).

Like Joseph, we also must be reminded that faith means loving someone enough to not judge him or her and cast  them aside. Instead, we must trust that God is at work in that person's life. Joseph, instead of walking out on the relationship, believed God's promise and stuck with it in spite of the circumstances.

Why do we always associate Christmas with home? Many of

our best memories are built around being home at Christmas. I remember the Christmas tree with presents under it. The Christmas carols I would sing with my brother and sisters on Christmas Eve, and then how we would go home after the Children's service and open those presents. I felt so at home.

Perhaps Augustine expressed this feeling best in his prayer, "Thou have made us for thyself, and our hearts are restless until they rest in Thee." At Christmas we see that the door between heaven and earth is opened to the point we can be at home with our Heavenly Father.

The German poet Holderin has written of the essential homelessness of all of us. This is our inability to ever feel completely at home in this world. "There is always a longing, a yearning for something more, for something beyond, for a life we can suspect but cannot touch. It's this homelessness that haunts the works of our greatest writers, musicians, and artists."

They know that our humanity is so limited that there is a mystery of that which lies beyond us. It lures, seduces, draws, and teases us. In the Christmas story God himself is getting in touch with us through a baby born in Bethlehem. He is saying, "Here is my gift of love. You have a home with me."

Jesus himself later said, "My Father's house has many rooms; if that were not so, would I have told you that I am going there to prepare a place for you? And if I go and prepare a place for you, I will come back and take you to be with me that you also may be where I am" (John 14:2-3).

At Christmas we should all feel so at home that whatever we face in this world, we know we don't have to be afraid because we have a home forever with Christ. This reality is very difficult for those who close their hearts and minds to accepting the needs of others. They expect God to project the same coldness and hardness of heart that they do.

Christmas is the celebration of being contacted by God and given a chance to make some better decisions about our lives. God has reached out to us and said, "I love you so much that I gave My one and only Son that whoever believes in Him will not perish but have eternal life" (John 3:16 paraphrased).

Now it is time for us to come home to our creator and tell Him, "I'm glad God that you have gotten in touch with me through Jesus. I do want to come home to you. Through the power of the Holy Spirit, I'm going to make some very important changes in my life. Thank you for your gift of Jesus. I am receiving Him now and coming home into your presence.

Chapter Ten – The Christmas Gift of Mercy

Christmas is the story of God's mercy, which is new every morning through Christ. I was meditating on that as the minister on the radio was sharing from Lamentations 3:23 where it says, "God's mercy is new every morning." Then

he went on to say, "Think about how much mercy God has shown you by multiplying the number of years old you are by 365 days. That number is the minimum amount for how many times God has shown you mercy in your life."

I was so busy figuring out this amount, when I suddenly noticed flashing red lights in my rear-view mirror. I had been so excited about all this mercy God had extended to me through sending the Christ of Christmas that I had totally forgotten about the speed limit.

When I pulled over an officer walked up to my car announcing, "You were going 78 miles per hour in a 60 mile an hour zone." As he spoke, I thought the speed limit was 70 or at least 65 miles per hour. Then he looked at me and declared, "You're the reverend". Even though I had been going with the flow of the traffic that was no excuse. I was guilty as charged.

As he took my license back to his car it seemed like an eternity before he returned. I knew I couldn't afford to add more to my credit card but what else could I do. My bank account was empty.

When the officer returned, he handed me my license and then said, "I'm giving you a warning ticket. Keep up the good work." I was almost in a state of shock as I replied,

"Thank you officer for extending the mercies of God". Then I took his hand and shook it as I said, "God bless you".

When I proceeded down the highway, I was not only very carefully observing the speed limit but celebrating the mercy of God that had just been extended to me.

The time has come for us to celebrate an even greater gift of mercy that God has given us. Matthew 1:23 declares that Isaiah 7:14 has been fulfilled. "The virgin will conceive and give birth to a son, and they will call him Immanuel' – which means, 'God with us.'" This means God has had mercy on us for "God is with us." He has chosen not to judge us for our sins but to extend His mercies, which are new every morning. God has had such great mercy upon us, "that He gave His one and only Son, that whoever believes in Him shall not perish but have eternal life" (John 3:16).

Now, like the wise men we have every reason to celebrate – "When they saw the star, they were overjoyed. On coming to the house, they saw the child with His mother Mary and they bowed down and worshipped Him. Then they opened

their treasures and presented Him with gifts of gold and of incense and of myrrh" (Matthew 2:10, 11).

Many don't truly celebrate Christmas because they can't see the mercies God that have been extended to them by sending His only begotten Son. How we need our eyes opened to the real meaning of Christmas where we can truly see that Christmas is more than just a baby in a manger. Jesus said in Matthew 13:16, "Blessed are your eyes because they see, and your ears because they hear." If we are going to truly celebrate Christmas this year, we need God to open our eyes of faith to who Jesus is and what He has done for us.

In 2 Kings 6:15 we see that Elisha's servant woke up one morning and discovered that they were totally surrounded by enemy soldiers. When the servant panicked and cried out, "Oh no, My Lord, what shall we do?" Elisha responds, "Don't be afraid," the prophet answered. Those who are with us are more than those who are with them. And Elisha prayed, 'Open his eyes, Lord, so that he may see.' Then the Lord opened the servant's eyes, and he looked and saw the hills full of horses and chariots of fire all around Elisha" (2 Kings 6:16, 17).

When our eyes of faith are opened, we are assured in the depths of our soul that no matter what the circumstances may be, we do not need to be afraid. Joseph, after being told this in Matthew 1:20, believed, and God provided for him. In this case God used the wise men to share gifts to finance Joseph, Mary, and the baby Jesus' trip to Egypt "where he stayed until the death of Herod."

(Matthew 2:15). In the same way you can also truly celebrate life when you choose not to fear but instead go forth by faith knowing that God has extended His mercy to you and will protect you.

In Luke 1:13 we see Zechariah being told to not be afraid. Mary is told the same thing in Luke 1:30, "Do not be afraid, Mary, you have found favor with God". The reason you and I don't have to be afraid is because we have experienced the mercy and favor of God. Because this mercy is not a result of anything we have done it is called grace. This grace is God's free gift resulting from His infinite love. It is not for us to question this unmerited mercy but to celebrate the fact that it exists "for nothing will be impossible with God" (Luke 1:37 ESV).

Just as Mary celebrated the miracle of Christmas and declared, "I am the Lord's servant," Mary answered. "May your word to me be fulfilled" (Luke 1:38), we are also invited to receive this miracle of mercy and let Christ be born within us. In Mary's case it was in the incarnation. In our case it is the re-creation. "Therefore, if anyone is in Christ, the new creation has come. The old has gone, the new is here!" (2 Corinthians 5:17).

> Therefore, if anyone is in Christ, the new creation has come. The old has gone, the new is here!"
> 2 Corinthians 5:17

When this recreation has taken place in our lives, we will join Mary in the celebration and declare, "My soul glorifies the Lord and my spirit rejoices in God my Savior, for He has been mindful of the humble state of His servant. From now on all generations will call me blessed, for the Mighty One has done great things for me – holy is His name" (Luke 1:46-49).

This Christmas lets truly celebrate the mercy that God has extended to us because, "He has brought down rulers from their thrones but has lifted up the humble. He has filled the hungry with good things but has sent the rich away empty" (Luke 1:52, 53). Let Christmas be a time of knowing that God has promised to give us mercy and will, "Rescue us from the hand of our enemies and enable us to serve Him without fear" (Luke 1:74).

There is mercy and hope for our Savior has been born. This realization touches every area of our lives. We are able to say, "Thank you Father that I have your mercy through Jesus Christ. I am no longer a victim because you have made me a victor. Your mercy is opening for me doors of opportunity both now and throughout all eternity. Yes, "You are my portion, Lord; I have promised to obey your words. I have sought your face with all my heart, be gracious to me according to your promise" (Psalm 119:57-58).

When you are living in the reality of God's mercy, you

begin to have your eyes opened and you see God's goodness in every area of life. As your eyes are opened to the reality of the mercy of God demonstrated through the sending of Jesus Christ you will naturally respond as the shepherds did. "When they had seen Him, they spread the word concerning what had been told them about this child and all who heard it were amazed at what the shepherds said tocei.....ve Grough the Living

Therefore prepare your minds for action; discipline yourselves; set all your hope on the grace that Jesus Christ will bring you when he is revealed.
1 Peter 1:13

Christ share it with others. Celebrate the fact the Savior has come and now, "with minds that are alert and fully sober, set your hope on the grace to be brought to you when Jesus Christ is revealed at his coming" (I Peter 1:13).

Simeon, an old man in the temple did not experience the mercy of God provided through the resurrected Christ as you and I can today yet, "Simeon took Him (as a little baby) in his arms and praised God, saying: 'Sovereign Lord, as you have promised, you now dismiss your servant in peace. For my eyes have seen your salvation, which you have prepared in the sight of all nations" (Luke 2:28-31).

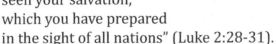

Now let the Lord open your spiritual eyes, declaring, "According to your faith let it be done to you" (Matthew 9:29). A Savior has come. Celebrate the new mercy He has given. Believe that God has demonstrated His love for you by the sending of His Son. Receive this good news of great joy and believe that God's mercy has been poured out upon you through Jesus, your Immanuel. As you turn from sin and unbelief to the resurrected Christ begin to live and celebrate life. Do not be afraid. Celebrate the faith and mercy God has provided through the Christ of Christmas.

Chapter Eleven – Receiving Your Christmas Miracle

Are you in need of a Christmas miracle? Are you under attack? Do things look hopeless? There just doesn't seem to be a logical solution. Then in order to survive you must not only turn to God's word but live in it daily.

The Celebration of Christmas is the celebration of divine lovemaking. The angel explained this to Mary in Luke 1:35, "The Holy Spirit will come on you, and the power of the Most High will overshadow you. So, the Holy One to be born will be called the Son of God." What a miracle! What a gift!

Mary after hearing she was going to give birth, declared in Luke 1, "My soul glorifies the Lord, and my spirit rejoices in God my Savior" (Verses 46-47). "He has performed mighty deeds with his arm; he has scattered those who are proud in their inmost thoughts. He has brought down rulers from their thrones but has lifted up the humble. He has filled the hungry with good things but has sent the rich away empty."

The miracle of Christmas involves the miracle of the incarnation. This is where Jesus was conceived through the power of the Holy Spirit without the involvement of a human father (Luke 1:35). As a result, God the Son became a human being without giving up His deity. When we accept the reality of this miracle, we are then able to realize that the celebration of Christmas is the celebration of God's miracle power.

The celebration of God's miracle power means that when things look impossible, we are reminded that Jesus is the living miracle who causes us to confess that "all things are possible for those who believe" (Mark 9:23).

In order to experience this miracle, we must understand that we can't give in to fear. That is why over and over in the Christmas story we are told to, "fear not". The angel said to Mary, "Fear not, Mary. . . The Holy Ghost will come upon you, and the power of the Highest shall overshadow you. . . For with God nothing shall be impossible" (Luke 1:30, 35, 37).

As we struggle with God's promise and plans for our lives, we need to let His "fear not" reassure us that His power and provision are sufficient to meet every need. In Luke 2:10-11 we see the angel telling the shepherds, "Do not be afraid. I bring you good news that will cause great joy for all the people. Today in the town of David a Savior has been born to you; he is the Messiah, the Lord."

Just as the shepherds were told, even so we must also be reminded that in spite of the circumstances, miracles are often born in the least expected times and places! Joseph was reminded of this when the angel told him, "Joseph son of David, do not be afraid to take Mary home as your wife, because what is conceived in her is from the Holy Spirit."

Like Joseph, we also must be reminded that faith means loving someone enough to not judge him or her or cast them aside. Instead, we trust that God is at work in that person's life. Joseph, instead of walking out on the relationship, believed God's promise and stuck with it in spite of the circumstances.

From the divine love making comes forth not only one

child but the redemption of each one who lets the Holy Spirit come upon them and the power of the Highest overshadow them. This is possible because this one who was born, Jesus, died for our sins and rose from the dead. Those who receive this power from on high do so as Mary did declare, "Behold, I am the handmaid of the Lord; let it be to me according to your word" (Luke 1:38).

The result is the Holy Spirit comes upon the surrendered heart and the power from on high fertilizes the egg of the Christ who lives within. New birth results in one who, like Mary, surrenders to the overshadowing of the power of the Highest and the miracle of Christmas unfolds once again. God comes upon us, covering us with His power and presence to the extent we are swallowed up in His love. Love beyond description. Love so divine, so powerful that it takes millions of created species resulting from that love to sing His praise daily.

God desires to empower us, overshadow us, and rapture us into His presence until we burst forth from the limitations of time and space. When we are involved at this point in divine love making, we will understand when the angel says, "The Holy One who is to be born will be called the Son of God." Christ, the hope of glory, the miracle of Christmas is born within each one of us. As verse 37 says, "For no word from God will ever fail." No wonder Mary bursts forth in song in verses 46-56 beginning with the words, "My soul glorifies the Lord and my spirit rejoices in God my Savior." She has experienced in its truest form divine lovemaking.

This Christmas, let the Christmas lights remind you that, "God is light, pure light; there's not a trace of darkness in him. If we claim that we experience a shared life with him and continue to stumble around in the dark, we're obviously ly-ing through our teeth—we're not living what we claim. But if we walk in the light, God himself being the light, we also experience a shared life with one another, as the sacrificed blood of Jesus, God's Son, purges all our sin" (I John 1:5-7 The Message Bible).

Right now, we must be willing to receive the Christmas Miracle that God provides. Let us believe and fear not, knowing that the wonder of the Christmas miracles of Christ's resurrection is here upon us. Christ is risen and it is His light that has driven the darkness from our lives.

Peter Keift writes in, *Everything You Wanted to Know About Heaven,* "This spiritual intercourse with God is the ec-stasy hinted at in all earthly intercourse, physical or spiritu-al. It is the ultimate reason why sexual passion is so strong, so different from other passions, so heavy with suggestions of profound meanings that just elude our grasp."

Catherine of Siena prayed, "O fire surpassing every fire because you alone are the fire that burns without con-suming! Yet your consuming does not distress the soul but fattens her with insatiable love."

God's divine lovemaking has no limits. Madame Guyon described the dynamic experience this way, "I slept not all night, because Thy love, O my God, flowed in me like deli-cious oil, and burned as a fire. . . I love God far more than the most affectionate love among men loves his earthly attachment."

Experiencing God's divine love making is not just about ourselves. Saint John of the Cross declared, "I abandoned and forgot myself; all things cased; I went out from myself leaving my cares forgotten among the lilies.

The resurrection of Christ causes us to realize that "Ev-erything is possible for one who believes" (Mark 9:23).

Just as Mary celebrated the miracle of Christmas and declared, "I am the Lord's servant," (Luke 1:38), we are also invited to receive this Christmas miracle and let Christ be born within us. As this happens, we will know we can do all things through Christ who dwells in us.

In Mary's case, the Christmas miracle was the incarnation. In our case it is the re-creation. "If anyone is in Christ, the new creation has come. The old has gone, the new is here!" (2 Corinthians 5:17). When this re-creation has taken place in our lives, we shall join Mary in the celebration and declare, "My soul glorifies the Lord and my spirit rejoices in God my  Savior, for he has been mindful of the humble state of his servant. From now on all generations will call me blessed, for the Mighty One has done great things for me – holy is His name" (Luke 1:46-49).

Instead of fearing the uncertainty of the future lets experience the miracle of Christmas knowing that God has promised "to rescue us from the hand of our enemies, and to enable us to serve Him without fear" (Luke 1:74).

Today is the day for us to experience the miracle of Christmas and the hope the risen Christ brings. The realization of this touches every area of our lives. We can say, "Thank you Father that I have your favor through Jesus Christ. I am no longer a victim because you have made me a victor. Your favor is opening for me doors of opportunity both now and throughout all eternity."

Then go on and declare, "You are my portion, Lord; I have promised to obey your words. I have sought your face with all my heart; be gracious to me according to your promise" (Psalm 119:57-58). When we are living in the reality of God's favor, we begin to have our eyes opened and we see God's goodness in every area of life. As a result, we will thank Him daily for His favor.

Thank God today for Jesus and celebrate the fact the Savior has come, "...set your hope on the grace to be brought to you when Jesus Christ is revealed at His coming" (I Peter 1:13).

Simeon an old man in the temple declared, "Sovereign Lord, as you have promised, you may now dismiss your servant in peace. For my eyes have seen your salvation, which you have prepared in the sight of all nations" (Luke 2:28-31).

Now as our Risen Lord opens our eyes to the Christmas miracle He has for us, may we believe that "According to your faith let it be done to you" (Matthew 9:29).

The time has come for us to turn from sin and unbelief to the resurrected Christ. When we do that, we will begin to live and experience our Christmas miracle today and for all eternity.

75

Chapter Twelve – Overcoming the Baby Jesus Syndrome

Every Christmas season Christians around the world are encouraged to worship the Baby Jesus. Through manger scenes, songs, and sermons the hearts and minds of millions are focused on the Baby while they let fear immobilize them when it comes to boldly stepping out in faith and working for justice and compassion.

Pastor Harold C. Warlick, Jr. refers to this as the Baby Jesus Syndrome. He says "It looms as one of the most universal perversions of the Christmas mind set. Overlooking the fest with notions of docility, innocence and helplessness of infancy gives much of the Christmas celebration an amoral and sentimental tone. A balanced approach to the celebration of the incarnation must put first the man Jesus who demands a mature commitment from his followers."

Can we really celebrate Christmas in anything less than a hypocritical fashion when we refuse to respond to the growing number of homeless people in our midst? As a result, many a child is laid in a manger of homelessness in our communities because there is no room for him or her at the inn. This Christmas, the manger in a room shared with three families because there is no apartment available that they can afford. At other times this manger is found in a vacant building, the back seat of a car, a bus stop, or a host of other places, none of which could be referred to as home... because there is no room at the inn. When one tries to move that manger into a particular neighborhood, inevitably, a handful of people intoxicated with fear will attempt—like

Herod did—to dispose of the child.

The very presence of the child, in the mind of the fearful, poses a particular threat to their kingdoms and property values. That the Christ Child appears today in the body of a homeless man, woman or child is without dispute when one is familiar with Matthew 25:31-46. Yet all too frequently our fears cause us to sing "Oh come let us adore him" in our church buildings one hour and then lock our Lord out when He comes on a cold winter night in the form of a homeless person in search of a place to stay.

The word Sanctuary, when applied to the church, used to mean a place where the poor, the homeless and the oppressed could go to for direct help (not a refer- ral). If we allow fear to  imprison us, soon this word sanctuary will mean to us a place where we can escape from the poor, the homeless and the hungry. Such an interpretation is totally foreign to the Scriptures (See Isaiah 58:6,7; Leviticus 25:35-38; Genesis 18:1-15; Matthew 25:35-45; Luke 14:12-14; Romans 12:13; plus, a host of other places).

Perhaps it's time we once again listened to the angel's message to the shepherds found in Luke 2:10-12 when he said, "Do not be afraid. I bring you good news that will cause great oy for all the people. Today in the town of David a Savior has been born to you; he is the Messiah, the Lord. This will be a sign to you: You will find a baby wrapped in cloths and lying in a manger."

In spite of such an appeal, many would still prefer a help- less baby who laid in a manger 2000 years ago to a Risen Christ who challenges us to confront the injustices in the world around us. Just as some are threatened by the sight of poor people of a different race greeting them outside their "Sanctuary" on a Sunday morning, even so, they feel uneasy when confronted by a grown Jesus who challenges His followers to reach out to the downtrodden. It is so much easier to "worship" a cuddly seemingly helpless little baby, than a Risen Lord who demands total commitment. Such worship stirs the emotions and desensitizes the conscience until one is quite content with their Gospel of Christmas Tokenism. This gospel allows them to dump their unwanted junk on the poor and then feel they have done their Christian duty.

Harold Warlick goes on to say, "Our infatuation with the baby tells us a great deal about ourselves. We worship the infant because we have not grown in our awareness of the Christmas revelation. At Christmas or any other time, Christians should worship the presence of a living God who demands justice."

Not only does a grown Jesus call us to repentance unlike no infant can, but He also desires to help us. His plea, "Come to me all you who are weary and burdened, and I will give you rest" (Matthew 11:28), is an invitation to experience His daily assistance as we walk down the road of life. It is the mature Risen Christ whose victory over death offers us freedom from fear and sin and then invites us to experience  the reality of heaven itself. This is something that the Baby Jesus Syndrome alone can never provide. Although the crib and traditional Christmas images may help dramatize the humanity of Christ, we must not stop there. The time has come for us to examine whether our Christmas celebration causes Christ to revert to childhood or challenges us to accept our Risen Lord and move by faith with Him into the hurting world around us.

Revelations 12:11 tells us how believers can defeat Satan as he engages in all outward warfare to defeat and destroy them. Verse 11 says, "They triumphed over Him by the blood of the Lamb and by the word of their testimony; they did not love their lives so much as to shrink from death."

In order to overcome Satan by the blood of the lamb, who is Jesus Christ, and the word of our testimony, that He is Lord of our lives we must:

#1-Realize we need a Savior and accept the fact that this Savior has come.

#2-Accept the fact that this Savior is Christ the Lord whose lordship we can turn to and trust daily in spite of whatever overwhelming obstacles Satan may throw at us.

#3-We must then grow in our faith as we read the Bible and have personal daily contact with that babe wrapped in rags, be he homeless, elderly, hungry, etc. This involves getting to know those in need as people, not only by name, but also to the extent that they become our brothers and sisters. Then 1 John 4:18, which says that perfect love casts out all fear, will go to work in our lives.

My prayer is that this Christmas our community will see the homeless and hurting in our midst, not as people to be feared, but as a special gift that God has blessed us with to remind us of His presence. We are all like unlit torches waiting to be lit by the flame of God's Spirit. A graphic illustration of this occurred on the Day of Pentecost (Acts 2:1-3). When the Holy Spirit, promised by Jesus, appeared as flaming tongues of fire on the heads of his followers. The results? These men and women turned the world upside down with their testimony of God's desire to once again be in intimate fellowship with those who let Jesus Christ, the light of the world, kindle His Spirit, within them.

It is time for us to let God kindle the Real Spirit of Christmas in our hearts. Nothing else can satisfy but the fire of His love as it is shared with the hungry, the hurting and the homeless.

As we trim our tree this Christmas, we can rise above the meaningless custom of making a showy display that is quickly forgotten when the New Year begins. Instead, it can be a time for reflecting on the God who created Christmas. As we set up the tree (real or fake), we can remember that He is the Vine, and we are His branches (John 15:1-6).

As we string the lights across the branches, we can remember that we are to be the lights in the midst of a dark and hopeless world (Ephesians 5:8-13).

The crowning of the tree with the Shining Star can be our way of honoring the Bright Morning Star, Jesus Christ, whose light illuminates our lives (Revelation 22:16).

Then as we place our gifts under the tree, may we remember that we prove God's love to one another (1 John 4:7-12) as we let His love flow through us with acts of compassion and justice in a hurting world.

And finally, as we plug in the tree and its light fills the room, may this Scripture come to mind: "Never be lacking in zeal, but keep your spiritual fervor, serving the Lord" (Romans 12:11).

We can let our light shine even as Satan declares war on the saints, because we know we are more than conquerors through Christ who strengthens us (Romans 8:37).

Remember Revelation 12:11 tells us that they overcame Satan by the blood of the lamb (our Risen Lord Jesus Christ) and the word of their testament and did not love their lives to death. Christmas is celebrated not because Jesus was a baby but because, "In Him we have redemption through His blood, the forgiveness of sins, in accordance with the riches of God's grace" (Ephesians 1:7).

It is the blood of Jesus Christ which creates the scarlet thread of God's power to be woven throughout the Scriptures. As this war intensifies, we know we are further empowered by the Holy Spirit who fulfills the promises that God has given us in the Scriptures.

Along with these promises we also have the power of prayer. The Christ of Christmas tells us that as we overcome the Baby Jesus Syndrome through the power of the Holy Spirit, we are to, "Ask and it will be given to you; seek and you will find; knock and the door will be opened to you. For everyone who asks receives; the one who seeks finds; and to the one who knocks, the door will be opened" (Matthew 7:7-8).

What power Christ has given us through His coming at Christmas to touch a hurting world. What grace He has bestowed upon us to share help with the helpless and hope with the hopeless. Let us now overcome the Baby Jesus Syndrome and approach the throne of grace and pray at this hour with confidence. Hebrews 4:16 says, "Let us then approach God's throne of grace with confidence, so that we may receive mercy and find grace to help us in our time of need."

We can come to God's throne of grace with confidence once we have received and obey the Resurrected Christ of Christmas. Don't wait any longer. Ask Jesus Christ to be your Lord and Savior and then live a life of obedience to Him who has said, "Truly I tell you, whatever you did for one of the least of these brothers and sisters of mine, you did for me" (Matthew 25:40).

Chapter Thirteen – Celebrating the Hope that Christmas Gives

Fear is mounting worldwide. There is war in the Holy Land, Ukraine, and other places. The economies of the nations are shaking and crumbling. Violence is becoming more rampant. At this time, we are watching the words of Jesus found in Luke 21:25, 26 being fulfilled before us; "There will be signs in the sun, moon, and stars. On the earth, nations will be in anguish and perplexity at the roaring and tossing of the sea. People will faint from terror, apprehensive of what is coming on the world, for the heavenly bodies will be shaken."

The time has come for us to absorb God's promise of hope that the angel Gabriel spoke to Mary in Luke 1:30, 31 "Do not be afraid, Mary; you have found favor with God. You will conceive and give birth to a son, and you are to call him Jesus."

For the followers of Jesus there is a freedom of fear that passes all understanding. This freedom comes from surrendering fears, like Mary did, into the care of God. It means putting ourselves completely under His wisdom, power, provision and understanding.

This is the reason why we celebrate Christmas. If we do so, He will place a star of hope over our lives just as He did over the town of Bethlehem on that glorious night His Son was born.

In order to experience this star of hope we must believe the words that the Angel spoke to the shepherds in Luke 2:10-11, "Do not be afraid. I bring you good news that will cause great joy for all the people. Today in the town of David a Savior has been born to you; he is the Messiah, the Lord."

The shepherds were alone on a hillside hoping for a little light in the midst of Rome's oppressive power. Instead of a little light, our gracious heavenly Father went way beyond anyone's wildest dreams by sending Jesus who declared, "I am the light of the world; he who follows Me will not walk in darkness but will have the light of life" (John 8:12).

This light is further explained in Matthew 1:21 when Joseph is told by the angel in a dream not to be afraid to take Mary as his wife because, "She will give birth to a son, and you are to give Him the name Jesus, because He will save His people from their sins."

The reality of this fact offers hope to those of us who realize we have "sinned and fall short of the glory of God" (Romans 3:23). Yet even though we were sinners destined to hell, God loved us and came among us. That is the star of hope Christmas provides.

The symbols of Christ's gift of forgiveness and eternal life are

everywhere during the Christmas season. There are Christmas trees,

brightly decorated to remind us of the fact Jesus is the light of hope in a

dark world. The evergreen Christmas tree itself reflects life even as all the

other trees have lost their leaves.

The candy cane is the result of a candy maker who wanted to invent a candy that would share the hope that Christ provides. First, he used a hard candy because Christ

is the rock of ages. This hard candy was shaped so that it would resemble a "J" for Jesus or, if turned upside down, a shepherd's staff. He made it white to represent the purity of Christ. Finally, a red stripe was added to represent the blood of Christ shed for the sins of the world, and three thinner red stripes for the stripes He received on our behalf from the Roman soldiers. The flavor of the cane is peppermint, which is similar to hyssop. Hyssop is in the mint family and was used in the Old Testament for purification and sacrifice.

Christmas can be a time of hope, full of wonders and miracles, or it can be a time of hopelessness and depression. When we respond like Mary did in Luke 1:38, "let it be to me according to your word", we give God permission to let the star of hope shine in our lives.

The reason we often miss the hope that Christ provides at Christmas is because of misguided materialism which drives us into such a frenzied pace that turns the hope Christmas provides into a time of distress, depression, and hopelessness.

Christmas is the celebration of the hope Jesus Christ provides. It is revealed to us as we allow the Lord to move in our lives in a supernatural way at exactly the right time. Paul speaks of this in Galatians 4:4 when he says, "but when the set time had fully come, God sent His Son."

In the Christmas Story we see that Jesus came at just the right time. He came at a time when the transportation system of the Roman Empire paved the way for the gospel to be spread throughout the then-known world. The Greek culture had provided a universal language of Greek for communicating the gospel. As we reflect on God's perfect timing for the miracle of Christmas, we are reminded that He has a plan, a timing and a miracle for allowing everything to work out for good in our lives (Romans 8:28).

God's plan for our lives involves supernatural seasons.

We are reminded of this with the evergreen Christmas tree that continues to remain green in the cold winter months when most of the other trees have lost their leaves. In spite of the circumstances, we can have hope as we move forward with the certain rhythm of heavenly timing. We learn that as we pass through winter, spring, summer and fall that God has everything under control; for "There is a time for everything, and a season for every activity under the heavens" (Ecclesiastes 3:1).

Christmas teaches us that we can have hope as we look for God's perfect timing and recognize it when it comes. Jesus corrected those who noticed only the seasons but ignored the signs of the times of what God was doing in the world and in their personal lives (Matthew 16:3). In order to recognize such, we need to seek Jesus during this Christmas season and discover His power of supernatural seasons in our lives!

Christmas not only shows us God's supernatural timing, but also how He weaves signs, wonders, and miracles into everyday life as He fulfills His promises. The birth of Jesus Christ is a fulfillment of God's promise to His people to send a Savior. "The Lord Himself will give you a sign: Behold, the virgin shall conceive and bear a Son" (Isaiah 7:14).

The Christmas Story is full of the signs of hope which communicate heavenly information. For example, the shepherds were told that the Christ child would be a sign to them, (Luke 2:12) and the wise men were directed by the sign of a star (Matthew 2:9-10). The fulfillment of the prophecies through the birth of Jesus Christ remains a sign of hope to those who continue to trust God no matter what the circumstances might be. In the scriptures there are over 300 prophecies that were fulfilled when Jesus was born.

Isaiah, in one of his many prophecies that Jesus fulfilled, declared, "For to us a child is born, to us a son is given, and the government will be on his shoulders. And He will be called Wonderful Counselor, Mighty God, Everlasting Father, Prince of Peace" (Isaiah 9:6).

All over in the Christmas Story we see the hope that the wonderful work of God shows. Just as the announcement of Christ's birth woke Mary, Joseph, and the shepherds to the hope of this historical event, even so we can also be awakened. How we need God to deliver us from the superficial aspects of Christmas and awaken us to the

wonders of His love and hope revealed through the sending of His Son and the beauty of His creation.

"When we take up permanent residence in a life of love, we live in God and God lives in us. This way, love has the run of the house, becomes at home, and matures in us, so that we are free of worry on Judgement Day - our standing in the world is identical with Christ's. There is no room in love for fear. Well-formed love banishes fear. Since fear is crippling, a fearful life - fear of death, fear of judgement - is one not yet fully formed in love. We, though, are going to love - love and be loved. First, we were loved, now we love. He loved us first" (I John 4:17-19 The Message Bible).

Christmas is a time of love when God desires to work miracles in our lives. Reflecting on the miracle of Christmas causes us to realize that "Everything is possible for one who believes" (Mark 9:23). The miracle of Christmas involves the miracle of the incarnation where Jesus was conceived through the power of the Holy Spirit without the involvement of a human father (Luke 1:35). This made it possible for God the Son to become a human being without giving up His deity.

When we accept the reality of this miracle, we are then able to realize that the celebration of Christmas is the celebration of God's miraculous power of hope and love. This means that when things look impossible, we are reminded that Jesus is the living miracle who causes us to confess that "Everything is possible for one who believes" (Mark 9:23).

The fact is that as we try to have hope, we find ourselves frequently facing opposition, doubt, and fear. God's response throughout the Christmas Story is "fear not". The angel said to Mary, "Fear not, Mary... The Holy Ghost will come on you, and the power of the Most High will overshadow you... For no word from God will ever fail" (Luke 1:30, 35, 37).

As we struggle with God's promise and plans for us, we need to let His "fear not" reassure us that His power and provision are sufficient to meet every need. In Luke 2:10-11 we see the angel telling shepherds to, "Do not be afraid. I bring you good news that will cause great oy for all the people. Today in the town of David a Savior has been born to you; He is the Messiah, the Lord."

As God releases His signs, wonders, and miracles in our lives, we must accept them with believing hearts. If we let unbelief, cynicism, greed, or double-mindedness creep in, we will find ourselves missing out on the hope that the miracle of Christmas provides.

Just as Mary celebrated the hope of Christmas and declared, "I am the Lord's servant, may it be to me as you have said" (Luke 1:38), we are also invited to receive this Christmas miracle and let Christ be born within us. In Mary's case, it was in the incarnation. In our case, it is the re-creation. "If anyone be in Christ, they are a new creation. The old has passed away the new has come" (2 Cor. 5:17).

When this re-creation has taken place in our lives, we shall join Mary in the celebration of hope and declare, "My soul glorifies the Lord and my spirit rejoices in God my Savior, for He has been mindful of the humble state of His servant. From now on all generations will call me blessed, for the Mighty One has done great things for me - holy is His name" (Luke 1:46-49).

This Christmas let us truly celebrate the hope it provides for, "He has brought down rulers from their thrones but has lifted up the humble. He has filled the hungry with good things but has sent the rich away empty" (Luke 1:52-53). Instead of fearing the uncertainty of the future lets experience the miracle of the hope of Christmas knowing that God has promised "to rescue us from the hand of our enemies, and to enable us to serve Him without fear" (Luke 1:74).

Jesus Christ was born a homeless child and placed in a manger, "because there was room for them in the Inn" (Luke 2:7 NKJV). We will never truly feel the hope of Christmas or be at home in any place until we have made room in our heart for Jesus. We do this by letting the love of Christ flow through us as we reach out and help those in need.

Don't take God's blessing of the Living Christ for granted. Thank Him for Jesus and spread the hope that the true meaning of Christmas brings. Celebrate the fact the Savior has come and now, "with minds that are alert and fully sober, set your hope on the grace to be brought to you when Jesus Christ is revealed at his coming" (I Peter 1:13).

As we experience the hope that Christmas gives, we will stop living in fear and hopelessness. We will believe that God has demonstrated His love for us by the sending of His Son. It is believing that Christ has come, died for our sins, and rose from the dead that we have hope both now and for all eternity.

Chapter Fourteen – A Christmas Spirit that Changes Everything

Before Jesus was born, his mother Mary, upon hearing that she was going to give birth to the Savior declared, "He has brought down rulers from their thrones but lifted up the humble. He has filled the hungry with good things but has sent the rich away empty" (Luke 1:52-53).

The story of Jesus birth has Mary and Joseph travelling from Nazareth to Bethlehem to be part of the census decreed by Caesar Augustus. In the process they find themselves homeless because there was no room for them in the inn.

The only place they can find to stay is in a stable where Mary gives birth to Jesus and lays Him in a manger from which the livestock eat. This scene of Jesus being wrapped in rags, called swaddling clothes, born to a temporarily homeless couple, and laid in a manger creates a scene of subversion. It involves a Christmas Spirit that changes everything because the Lord of Lords and King of Kings is not born in the seat of imperial authority but the most humble of circumstances.

The plot thickens with the proclamation of the birth of Jesus. Instead of a royal decree going forth, a group of society's "second class citizens", shepherds, have an angelic presentation brought to them as they are living in the fields watching their sheep. There with the glory of the Lord shining around them the angel declares, "Do not be afraid, I bring you news that will cause great joy for all the people. Today in the town of David a Savior has been born to you; He is the Messiah, the Lord" (Luke 2:10-11).

The angel has in his proclamation transferred the title Savior, which is often used for the emperor, to a homeless child in a stable. A great company of heavenly hosts then appear to declare that the birth of this child will bring "peace to those on whom His favor rests" (vs. 14). All of this shifts the power of the emperor to the side, while bringing ordinary people to the center where they can receive the message of God's favor.

It is the Christmas Spirit that changes everything. For, "Today in the town of David a Savior has been born to you; He is the Messiah, the Lord."

Studying the book of Luke shows me that the arrival of Jesus has turned the world upside down. While the power brokers try to steal the homes of the poor and elderly in the name of economic development, and then drive the homeless out of the downtown areas, Luke proclaims in his gospel the good news that God has sent Jesus to turn the world's corrupt system upside down and inside out.

Luke loves to share the message how Jesus moves the high and mighty to the side, while society's marginalized (the homeless, widowed, poor, and elderly) are brought to the center.

After Jesus resisted the devil's temptation to take the easy road and become part of the world's system, He stands up in the synagogue and proclaims His solidarity with the poor, the prisoner,

the blind and the oppressed. In Luke 4:18, 19 Jesus quotes Is 61:1, 2 when He declares, "The Spirit of the Sovereign Lord is on me, because the Lord has anointed me to proclaim good news to the poor. He has sent me to bind up the brokenhearted, to proclaim freedom for the captives and release from darkness for the prisoners, to proclaim the year of the Lord's favor."

Then Jesus added, "Today this scripture is fulfilled in your hearing" (Luke 4:21).

Jesus is speaking of the poor, the homeless, the prisoners, the blind and the oppressed. These are the people who are not at the center of power and wealth. As a result of Jesus extending God's favor to society's rejects, those who considered themselves privileged feel rejected and displaced. Out of this sense of displacement hostility emerges, and the privileged ultimately turn on Jesus.

Jesus continued to change everything. "Looking at his disciples, He said, 'Blessed are you who are poor, for yours is the Kingdom of God. Blessed are you who hunger now, for you will be satisfied. Blessed are you who weep now, for you will laugh. Blessed are you when men hate you, when they exclude you and insult you and reject your name as evil, because of the Son of Man" (Luke 6:20-22).

Jesus not only talked the talk when it came to social justice, but he walked the walk. In Luke 9:58 Jesus said, "Foxes have dens and birds have nests, but the Son of Man has no place to lay His head." Jesus the homeless One was fully God, as well as fully man, who had come to give life and give it more abundantly to the marginalized.

Luke tells us in his marvelous Gospel that Jesus came to change everything, not only in theory but in reality. That is what experiencing the Christmas Spirit is all about. It would be so much easier to just spiritualize the baby, the angels, and shepherds to be just another story in a different time and place. But this year I can't do that and hope to get any real meaning out of Christmas.

After the "powers that be" shut down the New Life Evangelistic Center at 1411 Locust I struggled with anger and resentment toward those responsible. When I would see a "millennial with money" walking down that empty portion of Locust between 14th and 15th street I would feel bitterness rise up in me.

I would remember how the streets were once shared with people who were homeless but now, they

1411 Locust Street

were empty, with the exception of those who have money and dogs. I struggled with feelings of anger every time I passed Lucas Park at 14th and Locust and saw dogs playing where homeless women and children once sat and played.

I knew that I needed a Spirit of Christmas that will bring about a change in me. It was this realization that caused the inner struggle to begin. It was so much easier to associate with people who agreed with my point of view than it was to understand the fears and concerns of those who thought their lives were better off because they had gotten rid of "those homeless people." This understanding did not call for my silence in the face of this injustice, but for me to enter the world of those I considered the perpetuators of injustice and listen to their concerns. From such listening I began to pray that reconciliation would come.

It is this Spirit of Christmas that awakens the realizations that those we differ with are fellow human beings that are made in the image of God, whom He also loves deeply.

Now as I pray for a revolution of love, I must let it begin with me. Unless I face the bitterness and unloving attitudes in my own life, I will never really be free to spread that love.

I can begin by letting the love of the Christ of Christmas cast out all fear and bitterness. This allows me to see those I differ from as fellow human beings with their own struggles and fears. As I do this, I know it will open the door to a deeper understanding of a Spirit of Christmas that changes everything.

The animosity between the political parties in America is like a cancer that is spreading across our beloved country and is even dividing families and individuals in our churches. We must now ask God to pour forth the Holy Spirit, the true Spirit of Christmas, into America like never before. When that happens, we will no longer be a nation that is divided but instead will become the United States of America.

If we want to really understand a Spirit of Christmas that brings about change, we need to look at how Mary, Zechariah, the angels, the shepherds, Simeon, and Anna, all expressed it in Luke 1 and 2.

Mary shows us that having a Christmas Spirit leads to social justice. She declares, "His (God's) mercy extends to those who fear Him, from generation to generation. He has performed mighty deeds with His arm; He has scattered those who are proud in their inmost thoughts. He has brought down rulers from their thrones but has lifted up the humble. He has filled the hungry with good things but has sent the rich away empty" (Luke 1:50-53).

Zechariah's expression of the Christmas spirit declares that God makes righteousness and justice possible, "because of the tender mercy of our God, by which the rising sun will come to us from heaven to shine on those living in darkness and in the shadow of death, to guide our feet into the path of peace" (Luke 1:78-79).

The angels proclaimed the Christmas spirit when they declared, "Glory to God in the highest heaven, and on earth peace to those on whom his favor rests" (Luke 2:14). Once the shepherds experienced this joyful proclamation of the angels, they took direct action to proceed to first seek the source of the spirit of Christmas, the Christ child. Then they told everyone about it (Luke 2:15-18).

When Simeon saw the Christ child, he was so moved by the Spirit that he declared, "Sovereign Lord, as you have promised, you may now dismiss your servant in peace. For my eyes have seen your salvation, which you have prepared in the sight of all nations: a light for revelation to the Gentiles, and the glory of your people Israel" (Luke 2:29-32).

Eighty-four-year-old Anna after seeing Jesus also gave thanks to God and told everyone about the child. Experiencing the Christ of Christmas causes us to thank God and then share in word and deed the hope that the spirit of Christmas provides.

How we need our spiritual eyes and ears opened to the real meaning of Christmas. When that happens, we will see and appreciate the Christ child. Jesus said in Matthew 13:16, "blessed are your eyes because they see, and your ears because they hear."

Having a Christmas spirit that changes everything involves total trust in the Christ of Christmas who declared, "I

Matthew 13:16, "blessed are your eyes because they see, and your ears because they hear."

am the way and the truth and the life. No one comes to the Father except through me" (John 14:6).

Because of the Christ of Christmas, we have found favor with God. Because this favor is not a result of anything we have done, it is called grace. It is God's free gift resulting from His infinite love. It is not for us to question this un-merited favor of grace but to celebrate the fact that it exists because "God is love" and "No word from God will ever fail" (Luke 1:37).

Just as Mary celebrated in the spirit of Christmas and de-clared, "I am the Lord's servant,' Mary answered, 'May your word to me be fulfilled" (Luke 1:38), we are also invited to receive this Christmas spirit that changes everything and let Christ be born within us. In Mary's case it was in the incarnation. In our case it is the re-creation. "If anyone is in Christ, the new creation has come. The old has gone, the new is here!" (2 Corinthians 5:17).

When this re-creation has tak-en place in our lives, we shall join Mary in the celebration and de-clare, "My soul glorifies the Lord and my spirit rejoices in God my Savior, for He has been mindful of the humble state of His servant. From now on all generations will call me blessed, for the Mighty One has done great things for me-holy is His name" (Luke 1:46-49).

We will never truly feel the spirit of Christmas until we receive God's gift of grace given through the Christ of Christmas. This involves letting Jesus be our Lord and Sav-ior to the extent we reach out and help those in need. "For it is by grace you have been save, through faith – and this is not from yourselves, it is the gift of God – not by works, so that no one can boast. For we are God's handiwork, created in Christ Jesus to do good works, which God prepared in advance for us to do" (Ephesians 2:8-10).

Chapter Fifteen – The Secret to Having a Merry Christmas

For many, Christmas is not a time of joy. Christmas memories which caused them to remember the seasons of the past, now haunt them with the reality that those they shared these good times with are no longer present. Christmas can easily become a time of depression unless they strive to do what I Thessalonians 5:16 says, "Rejoice Always".

To be honest there are a lot of reasons I can think of not to rejoice and have a Merry Christmas. In fact, if I'm not careful I will actually allow the door of depression to open and before long I find myself consumed with worry, discouragement, and frustration. The trouble is such a response cannot only become self-destructive but habit forming as well.

The alternative is to strive to have a Merry Christmas by meditating on the gift God has given us at Christmas. This involves more than just thinking about a baby in a manger, but what a gift that particular baby is and what He has done for us.

In order to have a Merry Christmas, let us ask the Holy Spirit to help us receive the gift of Christmas, and ground us in the scriptures that are joy filled truths. That list of truths include:

1.   Christmas reminds us of the reason the gift of Christmas is called Immanuel (God with Us) (Matthew 1:23).

2.   Having a Merry Christmas involves accepting the fact that God is for us.

3.   Christmas is the celebration of God's gift to us explained in John 3:16, "For God so loved the world that He gave His one and only Son, that whoever believes in Him shall not perish but have eternal life."

4.   Our debt of sin has been paid for and death has been conquered through Jesus' death and resurrection.

5.   Because of the death of God's only Son, Jesus and His resurrection, Heaven is our eternal home.

As we await heaven, how do we go on living in a world intoxicated by its lust for power without becoming disillusioned to the point where we no longer dream or have hope? God's response to this world that is intoxicated by its lust for power, is powerlessness. God chose to enter into human history as hope wrapped in a little baby. In this tiny powerless baby, who is completely dependent on its parents, we discover hope in the midst of our disappointments and the ability to dream again. That is the mystery of the incarnation. God became human, to break through the walls of power in total weakness and in the most hopeless of situations place a dream within our hearts. How does the story end? On a cross, where the same human person hangs naked with nails through his hands and feet.

The powerlessness of the manger has become the powerlessness of the cross. People jeered at him, laughed at him, spit in his face and shouted: "He saves others, he cannot save himself! If he is the King of Israel, let him come down from the cross now, and we will believe in him" (Matthew 27: 42).

Jesus is the celebration of hope, which He proved through His resurrection from the dead. His coming was prophesied to bring a social revolution where his

Kingdom would turn things upside down:" The mighty would be brought low, the rich sent away empty, the poor exalted, the hungry satisfied" (Luke 1: 52-53).

Jesus identified himself with the weak, the outcast, the downtrodden; the ones who have lost their ability to dream. His Kingdom undermines all economic systems that reward the rich and punish the poor. Jesus gives hope to the helpless, hurting, and homeless. In (Luke 6: 24-25) Jesus declared, "Woe to you that are rich for you have received your consolation." Woe to you that are full now for you shall hunger. He sets free those whose only dreams consisted of getting more money and things. Luke 12:15 says, "Take heed and beware of all covetousness; for a man's life does not consist in the abundance of his possessions."

Because of the life death and resurrection of Jesus Christ no matter how poor, homeless, or sick you may be, you can dare to dream again of life now and for all eternity. You can have hope in spite of your failures because Christ is risen.

As we get older, and our bodies get weaker it becomes increasingly critical that we are fully persuaded that God is able to make our impossible dreams a

Abraham was, "Fully persuaded that God had power to do what He had promised."

reality. Moses had to learn this as he was called forth at the age of eighty to deliver the children of Israel from captivity Abraham had to accept the fact that God was able to make him the father of a great nation when he was over ninety years of age. Romans 4:21 says that Abraham was "Fully persuaded that God had power to do what He had promised."

If you are going to accomplish that which God has called you to do you also must be fully persuaded that God is able to make your impossible dreams come true. You must accept the words that Paul declared in Ephesians 3:20 when he stated, "now to Him who is able to do immeasurably more that all we ask or imagine, according to His power that is at work within us."

In order to understand this power at work in us we must know what it means to be in Christ Jesus. II Corinthians 5:17 says, "If anyone is in Christ, he is a new creation; the old has gone, the new has come!" This power is a result of repenting of your sins and committing your life to Jesus and living daily under His direction. As a result, you are not just reformed, rehabilitated, or reeducated, but you are recreated (a new creation) living in union with Jesus Christ. "So then, just as you received Christ Jesus as Lord, continue to live in Him, rooted and built up in Him, strengthened in the faith as you were taught, and overflowing with thankfulness" (Colossians 2:6-7).

This Christmas dream the impossible dreams and know in the depths of your being that God loves you and will meet every need. This will happen as you renounce the god of this age who blinds the minds of those who refuse to believe the Word of God. As a result, "they cannot see the light of the gospel of the glory of Christ, who is the image of God. For God, who said, 'Let light shine out of darkness, made His light shine in our hearts to give us the light of the knowledge of the glory of God in the face of Christ. But we have this treasure in jars of clay to show that this all-surpassing power is from God and not from us" (II Corinthians 4:4, 6, 7).

If you are fully persuaded this Christmas that God loves you then there is no limit to what God can do through you.

Sure, you may encounter difficulties but "we do not lose heart. Though outwardly we are wasting away, yet inwardly we are being renewed day by day. For our light and momentary troubles are achieving for us an eternal glory that far outweighs them all. So, we fix our eyes not on what is seen, but on what is unseen. For what is seen, is temporary, but what is unseen is eternal" (II Corinthians 4:16-18).

Now this Christmas let the word of God go down deep into your heart until you are fully persuaded that God loves you and will meet every need you are facing. "Remember we live by faith, not by sight" (II Corinthians 5:6). "In the power of God: with weapons of righteousness in the right hand and in the left;" (II Corinthians 6:7).

When we are feeling depressed, Satan is right there to try to bring us further down by telling us how worthless we are. We can't afford to forget that faith in the resurrected Christ is the victory, which enables us to overcome the devil. As Revelation 12:11 says, "They overcame him (Satan) by the blood of the Lamb (Jesus) and by the word of their testimony; they did not love their lives as much as to shrink from death."

This overcoming is possible because of faith which causes us to dream the impossible dreams and know that God is able to meet every need. "For whatsoever is born of God overcomes the world: and this is the victory that overcomes the world, even our faith" (I John 5:4).

Remember, by being in Christ we are able to overcome the world because we are "a new creation; the old has gone, the new has come!" (II Corinthians 5:17). That verse is our theme here at New Life Evangelistic Center.

As we do this, we are able to dream the impossible dream and know that God is able to meet the need He did this for Daniel, David, Moses, Joshua and so many others and He will do it for you.

You and I must never forget that the gift of faith, which

the Christmas message proclaims allows us to dream impossible dreams. This faith is activated through the Word of God. "Faith comes from hearing the message, and the message is heard through the Word of Christ" (Romans 10:17).

When I am facing an impossible situation, I must at that moment send the "911 prayer" to the Living God, the Creator, Redeemer and Sustainer of heaven and earth. I will also get others to agree with me in prayer. We must never forget what the angel said to Mary in Luke 1:30, "Do not be afraid, Mary; you have found favor with God."

Now let us rise up from the beds of defeat, knowing that "this is the victory that has overcome the world, even our faith. Who is it that overcomes the world? Only he (or she) who believes that Jesus is the Son of God" (I John 5:4,5). Now the time has come for us to stop worrying and pray fully persuaded that God has everything under control and that "we are more than conquerors through Him who loved us" (Romans 8:37).

I want to encourage you this Christmas to dare to believe knowing that Jesus is able to save you and answer your prayers. Remember God can deliver you from the fiery trials and strengthen you. Christmas is the fulfillment of one promise after another along with example after example of how God is able. Let Him show you now by accepting by faith that, "...He is able to do exceedingly above what you can even ask or think" (Ephesians 3:20).

Because Christmas is so much more than just a baby in a manger Thessalonians 5:16-18 tells us to "Rejoice always, pray continually, give thanks in all circumstances; for this is

God's will for you in Christ Jesus."

We may not be able to control our circumstances this Christmas, but we can choose in spite of them to give thanks, pray continually and be joyful. That is God's will for us.

Jesus also expressed in Matthew 25:31-46 that God's will for us involves helping others. In spite of the fact that our Immanuel said, "Whatever you did for one of the least of these brothers and sisters of mine, you did for me", many instead at Christmas are giving gifts to everyone but the hungry, hurting, and homeless. The result is they never have a Merry Christmas.

The secret to having a Merry Christmas involves accepting the Immanuel, the Christ of Christmas. Then let His love flow through you into the lives of the homeless and hurting. New Life Evangelistic Center throughout the months of October, November, December, and January has a series of special events to provide individuals the opportunity to give. These events are provided not only to directly help those in need, but to allow the ones giving to have a Merry Christmas. Further information on these events can be found at www.newlifeevangelisticcenter.org or by calling (314) 421-3020.

The secret to having a Merry Christmas lies in receiving God's gift of His only Son (John 3:16) and then sharing this gift in word and deed with others. Without the love of God flowing in us and through us it is impossible for us to experience a Merry Christmas.

Christmas is celebrating the fact God loved the world so much that He gave His only begotten Son and now as children of God we are being given the opportunity to give. It is through giving that we receive.

Christmas is truly more than a babyology of sentimental feelings concerning a baby in a manger. It is accepting the fact that God is now with us and desires to let His love flow through us into the lives of others. As we do this, we will experience the secret of having a Merry Christmas each and every day of our lives.

I want to invite you to join the New Life Evangelistic Center staff and partners as we celebrate Christmas all year long at NLEC TV. When you receive the gift of NLEC TV at your app store, you will get free wholesome family television and inspirational radio. In addition, there is 24-hour streaming  of creation messages and videos. You can also watch classic movies, inspirational messages, Here's Help shows connect you with the poor and homeless, and much more!

Be sure you go to nlecstl.org or newlifeevangelisticcenter. org. There you will learn how your partnership with New Life Evangelistic Center is directly helping the poor and homeless around the world. You can send your Christmas gift to New Life Evangelistic Center to P.O. Box 473, St. Louis, MO 63166.

I invite you to visit us at 2428 Woodson Road in Overland, MO or at 806 N. Jefferson in Springfield, MO. For further information, call (314) 421-3020.

My prayer is that you and your family have a Very Merry Christmas, knowing that Christmas is more than celebrating a baby in a manger. Christmas is the celebration of the Son of God becoming human, and through His death and resurrection, providing us life both now and for all eternity.